THE RED WORD
IN THE
Blue MIND

THE RED WORD
IN THE
Blue MIND

Long Live the Possum

MARVIN THOMAS

Library of Congress Control Number: 2015911572
ISBN: Hardcover   978-1-5035-8755-7
                  Softcover   978-1-5035-8754-0
                  eBook   978-1-5035-8753-3

Print information available on the last page.

Rev. date: 09/16/2015

To order additional copies of this book, contact:
Xlibris
1-888-795-4274
www.Xlibris.com
Orders@Xlibris.com
714418

CONTENTS

Chapter I

The Passion of Poetry

Jewel 17: Let us use brevity in the delivery of speech,
instead of beating around the bush with lofty words
that are many, to do the work of a few.

(1st Love-Marvin W. Thomas versus the United States of America)

Is this hell where I dwell a place you go when you fail?
And then you feel you have nothing else only your soul for sale
I want to scream and yell, but it want do me no good
So I walk in, being shown where I should sit, but I stood
Knock on wood, as she came from the back with a jet black robe on
Looking 99% confident that I'm removed
of restraints all protection gone
Rich oil paintings and furniture hand carved
out of mahogany is in this den
I'm trying to look my best, she's about to judge me from 0-10
Got me a little nervous a special date makes it hard to anticipate
Family and friends came along to see us, to
make sure everything was straight
The smell of genuine leather and oak stained
varnish aroma filled the air
This scene is absolutely stunning, but this
place is trapped with much despair
So we are in cross examination both staring
deep into each other eyez, words I find
I said I felt like I was a good man, give me a chance of some kind
Then all became eerie with silence as she
made up her mind what 2 do
You sent me papers, so I waited a long time
and came a long ways just 2 see you
From a place where tormented souls guess
and wonder, I'm about to know
As her desire is to hold you like her 1st love and never let you go

Attacked by the Universe

Am I supposed to be dead fifteen times ago?
But the elements say so, that I must survive
Why is it so important that I stay alive sir?
My life has been a blur up until this point
I want the world to be a better place with or without me
No one wants, to see a future without them in it
Life will never quit or give up till its job is done
I run on and run on till I can't run no more
Feet soar and mentally tired trying to reach the end
Till I been to the end of the sand dunes of time.
There the star shines bright as the blinding light of God
No one applaud our finish on the great work that's been
Against all odds of the universe one must stand
Everything has been planned and couldn't gone another way
So I say once again I'm divinely prepared
To share with the world a gift carried inside
While others died in vain not seeing or knowing
As the universe slung them out of time, going away
Our purpose is the reason while some are here
And it's no escaping our destiny at hand
So to hell and back let us finish the task
Moving fast, and swiftly as we're under attack

Budget Inn

What seemed like a dark alley that smelled of piss and oil?
Located underneath the rusty balcony of this hotel foyer
There stands a skinny white whore bug eyed off the crack
With heroin and a syringe, plus a crack pipe in her backpack
Hid with a dirty change of panties and God only knows what else
To spread her legs in this stinking room, fumes reeking of death
Curtains constantly pulled back waiting for
the a traveler in the parking lot
Doors open as soon as he drives in, to be ushered into the spot
Give me what you got, since he don't got but seventeen fifty
Twenty was the going price, but both move in the game swiftly
She's been doing business all day and not a single condom to spare
Either she trust he got one, already got
something, or simply don't care
The owner knows what goes on, but late night traffic pays the bills
Folks actually live in this hotel and cook on open grill for meals
As their children play where there are broken
beer bottles and jagged cans
Unattended, and malnourished, snotty noses, dirty faces and hands
Creeps walk from far and near to get to the Budget Inn
Late night lips licking for the same rush
achieved when they first begin
The Budget Inn got torn down, but so many lives got destroyed
In the darkness of its shadows from destruction
its demons roared and roared
As passer-byes let the old abandoned parking-lot catches their eyes
And some may not have memories of the terror underneath it lies
I'll just say it was dark, murky and chaotic filled with sin
A hellish nightmare had often been at the Budget Inn

Burning Bush

When I first seen it, I was speechless, too far gone reach less, it
was nothing else left, but to bow down?
A burning bush all around my barefooted toes clutched the ground as
I'm found hidden in flames deep in it.
This soft voice calls my name, as sweet from the heat
pours down like stormy rain, I remain silent.
Fate it seems has me searching for a talent, driven through the
fire to feel what my heart desire.
In the bush it seems to scream take me home, because I've become
intimate with the secret parts.
Nodding my head and being welcomed to enter
wide open into this dark precious
place rarely seen.
In between two leaning towers, I stop for a moment
smelling the fragrance, then look on to
passionately continue.
All the men that's been through, neglected
this, never taking the time to notice
what's been here all along?
So I lift up strong through extreme heat, make eye contact and see
what can't be imagined?
Being engulfed and consumed from the flames in
the womb of the valley of intense peace.
Then at least I'll have had a little taste of heaven, a brief
encounter if extreme temperatures release my soul.

DE'JAVU

It's all been done before let's have a look again
A re-run of premonitions that has no certain end
Now it's feeling weird freaking you totally out
This awkward scene that you already know about
Errie sense as it's been done got you nauseous
As you become acutely aware proceed with caution
In this reality that's trying to catch up with you
You see it in slow motion as it appears through
All you can do is sit back and let it happen
It's no leaving, no escape we're all trapped in
As life unfold and if we happen to be there
Same realities, that will reveal to us and share
It's not a dream as we arrive on the same scene
Paranoia kicks in and we begin to know what it means
Heart beating fast, stomach is quizzy, just 2 know
That life's so fragil in any moment, we all can go
Out the window of our soul we can see
The thing that has happened many times before me
And it's has happened many times before you
It's just sometime we see it again before it happens
Dejavu

Dedicated to Vanessa Williams

Don't call me Friend

I thought the attraction was mutual as we dealt
Intimate conversations shared, I thought was heart felt
Didn't you see the way I melted in your eyez
As we had serious discussions, then you would say bye
You whisk away, my glassy eye stare, I more than care
You talked of your past guys in relationships all cheated
Now the one you with is suspect, and got you heated
Showed me where you lived and invited me to come
Gave me your phone number, what if I want some
Will you be angry if I ventured out to be seductive
Cause of your string along tactics that are so elusive
At times it seems like we're lovers, then other times sister and brother
Don't want to smother this out, I'll ride this 2 the end
Spend time with him then me, but don't call me friend

Henry's Grandson

He left my grandma alone in this twilight zone
I remember the day I would hear him say I'm going away
Me and Henry would sit under the porch and see the misery
I'm kicked out school; he would say I'm here to eat up all the food
He pray over food, Thank the Lord even if I
don't get another one but I hope I do
Please let me in late night, I've been out in the sin
2 my demise, before you died, I'll never forget that look in your eyez
Scratch your back is how we interacted and made contact
You kept a stash, that was full of cash and made it last
Something's up the road for me is what you say when I don't cut grass
I was shown after you was gone, I won't alone
Your hard work, sweat and tears brought me through the years
I knew you loved me, even when it went without saying
And caring 4 me even when I was growing up disobeying
Family and friends that forgot you, I'll never do the same
Henry was my grandfather; I'll never forget your name

Hero

Superman is the name of fathers on the lips of every child.
A role model to be proud of
No matter how horrific the truth was
I drank because my daddy drank
Life ant got time to paint a pretty picture
I ask my homie how you let the feds get cha
As he shows me photos of his precious seed,
Which is the most beautifulist thing in the world?
Does reality balls its fist up and hitcha
And cuss you out and makes you man up
Take its back hand and slap you into fatherhood before you ready
To get your first
Nothing under the sun is one, two, three, and four free.
Diapers every time he pee, shush baby about to go to sleep
Dodge the bullet ha! ha! A hero doesn't have to.
Responsibility of a kid is something that he'll laugh through
He doesn't' run from it, he'll run forward toward it.
At the pace of a speeding train.
How many men can say that they've faced adversities and
Still been there 4 a son or daughter needing a superman
Leap a building in a single bound just to say that I love you.
My father spoke it with his action, when I
was down and he came through
So when it's you vs the world and you get
sucker punched with a clear blow
Listen to the whispers yelling for you to get
up because you're somebodies hero

In a Prisoners Heart

As rivers flow upward from South 2 North in the Nile
So do the lips of my African face even in prison tend 2 smile?
It's love in my heart for the brother man that extends a helping hand
Showing those flipping burgers upon release won't fill life demands
Life is expensive and to sell your Nubian self-short is 2 fall
4 me to care enough to tell you is compassion, I love you all
We all prayed on dudes, called them victims,
took advantage of weakness
But with strength comes responsibility so
one must be low with meekness
Not too defensive and just listen as I also was hard headed one time
Once out of prison, network brothers, share resources use your mind
Listen, Listen, we can't all do the same thing;
bring your gut-wrenching story
And we'll chop it up some, you really
innocent, somebody told, poor me
You keep the floor; I'll listen as long as when it's my turn do the same
We should be shame 2 be in prison, some take pride they came
Saying that's crazy about everything, most
people in here are burnt out
Or we'll call him shell shocked after these events of this prison route
Like the people of Kemit the Berbers; the burnt face nation
Now they call this place Egypt with the Moorish man our relation
Are here now, as we come along ways, but got far to go to say
All my brothers and sisters let's keep running
up the hill looking a better way

In loving memory of Josephine Myrick

Knocking on Heaven's Door

When it rains it pores, washing dirt from out my sores
I'm outside getting drenched knocking on heaven's door
Drunk from the skunk hole, throw up on my expensive shirt
In my hair is filled with grass mixed with dirt
I must have fell along the way, because my tail ache and hurt
I stagger pissy in hell through a pathway, where evil men lurk
I know I smell like a liquor steel, but I hope that I get in
If I can make it from this shot house, I'll make amends for my sins
Let's pretend life's been perfect, love you if no one else
Why do we poison ourselves with liquor, put
ourselves in positions to get shot to death
I thank about it all as I fall on the clean bed spread my head spin
Laying there thinking how lucky I've been with a foolish grin
But I made it in, "Thank you my Lord".
And in the morning God will have for me sausage, grits and eggs
Instead of lying in the ally, I get to see a heavenly bed
Through eyes blood shot red, I see and Thank God I'm not dead
I had said I loved you, but now I know you love me more
I'll never forget what you done for me when I went
Knocking on Heaven's Door

Lonely At the Top

Occasionally I talk to myself cause there's no one else
to converse with on my level, what in the devil got into him;
one might say as they see my mouth move from a distant place
far away. It's not by chance or accident I've ascended to this
pinnacle, and still must rise to another higher
area, underneath God's blue skies.
I want look away from where I must go or even
regret where I'm at while I'm soar.
Only a few get me and are with me to the end.
It's like they've searched their entire lives for
me, now asking where I have been.
He who accompanies me on the other level is my friend.
He sees what I see, and can relate to the sacrifice that we had to make.
This place is lonely and it takes a lot to get here.
Exhausted people quit, and take breaks and cry for rest.
Here it takes a certain person who can handle
stress, and not easily be overwhelmed,
by one false move can risk losing it all.
However the cushion to the fall is where mediocrity
resides, not even close to the bottom.
We see a few inches as ohh what a drop
Nobody is beating the door down to get here.
I'll ask myself if there's no one else why is it lonely at the top?
Maybe what might stop most people from
reaching here is they can't let go of what's
Holding them behind
Not willing to redefine themselves in moment's revelations.
That's the way they are now it's keeping them from flying

Madness of Desires

Ohh how sweet are the pure flames of passion and desires
Rose colored fires burst from complex feeling to simplicity
A heart enraptured in a tug-a-war attempting to be discreet
Intense heat burning through pregnant clouds ready to rain
Out skies with tenderness of love so a sun can brighter shine
In the allurement of her charms, stars burst blind
So enchanting is the light that entices and appeals to the dark
A white elegant spark for eyez to gaze in a morning day
As the sky lay on the horizon set ablaze the high noon
Spooning with the back of the hill tops; shadows illuminate
In every crack and crevice a lite luster rush deeply in
Running away the modesty of unseen things underneath blackness
The blindness of fiery rage slide in between satin of night
To thrust forth crisp light; then ease off to sleep with sweet whispers.

Naked Conversation

I'm holding a conversation with no cloths on it
Well let me expose what supposed to go on it
Maybe its garments caught up in the moment who knows
But first let me ask do you really want it
Cause it sound so easy to put something on don't it
Well it depends on what you chose
Most empty holes get filled with a rack of lies
If you uncover those you'll find a uniform of truth
Covering bare hello's and goodbyes
So I've undressed this nakedness with my eyez
No more disguise you don't think I do, but I see you
This conversation might as well be having on see through
Well in my view now I realize
After all the article are gone
Now let the truth be known, as it peeped both
Ways and shown me its beautiful tone
I love you and keep in touch was standing there
Speaking softly missing me so much
Standing so bare and so naked alone
While others was surrounded by so much going on and on
With outfits of silence blown in my ear
The clothz are idol and meaningless, these are
the weights that need to disappear
And this is a naked conversation

Dedicated to Hillary Rodman Clinton

Osama Bin Laden dies

I have no feelings for this scumbag Osama bin Laden finally dies
On Sept. 11th 2001 al- Qaida Taliban terrorist took about 3000 lives
All I can taste is a sour victory, the killing of another man gone mad
In Pakistan Navy SEALS dropped in and put him in a body bag
Dropped his body in the ocean why should
I care he called her an infidel
That's no way to treat a lady, whose name
is Liberty, the day the towers fell
He had already bombed the World Trade Centers
in 1993, this time jet liners hit good
The world was in terror as they seen people
jump from the top where they stood
In 1998 he bombed 2 U.S embassies in Africa that killed 231 souls
And even after all this some ask was he unarmed,
when he was shot full of holes
Is al-Qaida focused on worldwide jihad, attack the west from the skies
With a 100,000 U.S and foreign troops in
their country Osama bin Laden dies
It took almost 10yrs for Uncle Sam to get
him; he wasn't crouching in a cave
He wasn't hidden in some distant place, but in
a compound near the city that was raid
Assault on a female has turned deadly, will this ever be tried again
Ramming your planes inside her buildings, so
I sent forth 72 special trained men
All I could feel was my vengeance, all I could see Afghan Taliban ties
It started with Bush ended with Obama
administration, Osama bin Laden dies

MARVIN THOMAS

Police Brutality

Mace in the face cause her eye balls to itch and burn
As her boyfriend is being choked out, and being told shut your mouth
Beat with a Billy club, as kicks and punches are snuck in
The cuffs are way too tight, cutting off circulation in his wrist
His girlfriend shouts and scream as police
punches her boyfriend bloody
Telling him to face down and don't move,
makes it impossible to breath
Leave my daddy alone as a little boy runs from the back crying
His fathers is shocked with a stun gun, a thousand volts to his head
With a mouth full of blood and slobber,
he gurgles, son go to your room
He's yanked up by the cuffs, and dragged
on his knees through the house
Why are the authorities so mad as neighbors
whisper and gather around?
Surrounded in the streets, their video cameras out taking footage
Young gang member's walk-up closer, but not too close to protest
As officers watch the scene carefully, trying to keep it under control
Someone hurls a bottle and they hurry to push the crowd back
The man face is beaten, bloody and swollen to unrecognition
Police bump his head at the top of the squad unit's door
Sorry about that buddy the police say in a humorous joking demeanor
As they pull off, the man turns and looks back through the window
With only one eye left to barley see his girlfriend and son.

Dedicated to Allah

Ramadan

Let me sit down read my Qur'an in this madness
In the prison common area where men call
each other niggaz, then start laughing
I'm in my chair reading passive till the devil
Iblis come up and sit beside me
Telling nasty jokes and showing lewd photos ohh how Satan rides me
After he's tried he goes on to the next, while T.V shows promote sex
Can't sit comfortably in my cell that's the 1st place homeboys check
The chapel gives me pleasure to go and meditate while I fast
Till a blasphemer peeps his head in the room, how long will peace last
Then out of nowhere he says I thank I'm going
to put in for a job as an orderly
Poor me, as he continues on to bore me with his entire life story
My stomach walls are touching; some self-restraint will do me good
On my Al Hajj of life I must sacrifice from
many Surah's I've understood
While degenerate brotherz claim to fast but eat right out in public
They use to put a cover on the door to hide, but
to do that now makes them feel insulted
Then come up to you when it's time to
breakfast and say peace brother
Ask for a date to eat then go back to the
ignorant, to laugh at each other
I stand alone to watch from a far, I'm not perfect but dag on
Shouldn't every participate be sincere, and
show more respect in the month of
Ramadan

MARVIN THOMAS

Dedicated to Stacy Thomas

Sea our Love

Rushing waves to the shore rustles and roars
Splashing and crashing against rocks and sandy beaches
Reaching out further than before more and more
Bashing and smashing each of us life lesson teaches
That the sea is beautiful and dangerous look and see
How the ocean in motion, turns and rolls over
After the laughter and screams of children playing
Saying to one another look at the lover lean on his shoulder
No bolder love than this than a wave that comes running
Smelling the salt in the air caught by a summer breeze
And the sun beams through its rays bright light shines
Blinding facial features on this coast of people walking
But all I see is you in our private time, moments of mine
You're brighter than any sun the one and true love
Of a different kind soothing my soul as oceans do
What was this feeling that has a taste of chill or cold
Unfold back these clouds and let Angels peep at you
And for the first time you might see what I see
A life long journey to sea our love through

Seduction

Seduction begin when men enter in
The presence of a woman that has sights on you to befriend
As always unknowingly; you thought your game was to win her
When every time in the end she was the one who forced you to dinner
She made herself available for you to look at
while she pretend not to notice
Then like a fly in a web she would spin captivated all of your focus
You was seduced to ask her, her name and
with a boyish grin came to see
That you might extend a warm welcome,
and in your arms she would be.
But when she spoke of her favorite place to
eat and then drink to her friend
You overheard and ran with what had been a
group of supplanted seductive words send
But you can tell if it was only sport, cause
men are hunted like wild beast
Because of the way she will look at you and
stare or if it's too long then it's a tease
If she looks down then it's one or two things that's in progress
Either she's afraid of finding mutual attraction
or wants to intensify the process
So as she distance herself in connection,
this drives the seduced man wild
And have him thinking it was all his idea, feeling like
the man but really being played like a child
The game is foul in fact; it's not a game she's not playing with you
The mission is pursue, overtake and then destroy your single hood.

Sinner

What made me like this, how did I get this way?
Why lies are in all I say, who can handle the truth?
It's a shame and a scandal they tell me I'm going 2 hell
Well I might as well sale my soul, if of hell they have proof
I vandalize everything I touch, my hands clutch the bible
Ripping pages out because it's reliable paper to smoke weed.
Then bite my fingernails till they bleed cause I'm paranoid
Mischievously move forward, to get the 5th of vodka I need
Now being relieved, I'm looking my wife best friend for sex
We're unprotected, and now- a-day who check for disease
Who's got time to be faithful, you got heart let's see it break
As I do whatever it take to capture it just to squeeze
Some say I'm a low down dirty snake I can live with that
In this life it a fact you either deceive or be deceived
The greed of money, sex, and drugs is such a sweet joy
A devilish mind lost, it's what I chose but what do you believe

Slaves Master's Daughter

Jim sees her peeping so he creeps in through the night
Keeping this rendezvous into the weekend
with the slave master's daughter
Uncle Tom caught her with him, for now there little secret
Sorry Tom, he had to see it, but he'll never smell it
She tells him, Jim is who she wants to be with, So Tom is going
To get yelled at. Maybe even beaten, cause
that's how the bearer of bad news
Get treating, but revenge on Jim is what he's seeking
By any means, Up in the cabin with the slave
master's daughter doing sexual things
What will the master say and do, kill Jim
for sure, maybe the daughter too
Tom goes through with it, and master breaks both of his arms
Jim hears and is on the run. Neighbors
gather together to hunt him down
With knives and guns, Before Jim left he kissed
her and looked into her blue eyes
Only to realize it will end in darkness but for a
few moons he enjoyed the blonde sunrise
He'll never find out what happens to her as he
head for the woods and see torches
And lanterns coming, so like a wild animal he running, With his
burlap sack cut off pants, bare footed. In this wooded scene, dark
and cold, but continually coming are relentless screams, I'm gonna
kill you nigger, he figures it's a no win, is this the end and then
Just like a scary movie he's surrounded, he's been found
Heart beating fast, cut and bruised, he go ahead and screams
To God cause it's time to die, Jim screams
are buried in the thick of the night,

MARVIN THOMAS

SNITCH

As a polite police passes a cigarette and a
bottle of water to calm his nerves
The way authorities talking make him think he got a way with words
Times served with his statement, and then
just show me where to initial
Forward the paperwork to the prosecutors to
the judge to sign makes it official
All the risk through this makes him unable to be on the block
Especially if the neighborhood gets wind
that I've been speaking to the cops
In jail all this walking back and forth
inmates know by now he's talking
He's telling them it's his lawyer, but so many lies he's getting caught in
Everybody knows that the weak, don't eat,
get their trays took in the slammer
And a snitch get fingers pointed like guns
the thumb pulls back the hammer
Inside the bullpen with the bed roll, other side
detainees put "S" signs in the windows
To signal the snitch to let others inmates know,
sorry C/O inside he cannot go
He's the states secret dagger informant, lethal
blow that causes his Co-D's to blow trial
So he checks his motion of discovery and
agrees to plea, cope out, no denial
Except responsibility as I do, I didn't snitch he just told the truth
We all might as well turn in the evidence,
admit it they got us with the proof
Loose lips sink ships and make the inmates
check off from one cell to the next

Agents get info and then throw you to the
wolves, inside it's no way to protect
As word get out that you can't keep your
mouth closed, and so you're exposed
No one wants a snitch around, people that
you don't know becomes your foe
And if he's lucky he want get killed in the
streets, only in jail trying to survive
In prison trying to stay alive as a snitch, as
they look into unbelieving eyes
Of mothers, son, or grandmother from the stand and say he did it
Yeah that's him with his finger pointed with
betrayal, it makes them admit it

So Sorry

I loathe the fact that I ask too much of God
When I'm not appreciative of what I already have
The fresh air I breathe and my perpetual heartbeat
Are the most essential components ever in life?
Yet foolishly I ask for money, good fortune, and a good woman
What a selfish arrogant bastard, I've become
Having the nerve to not say nothing, I mean nothing.
When I awake in the morning, so out of touch
Not even to have God on my inconsiderate mind
Without question I need to be severely punished
But how can I ask for a punishment reprehensibly
My absent mindless is probably worthy of death
As long as God don't with draw his love from me
I hope and pray that I can take whatever he gives
But if his mercy endures for all times and always
Then he will work with me a little while more
I'm so sorry God that I've been so intolerable ignorant
If I could ask for anything, it would be a better relationship
A Closer, more intimate and deeper passion.
I love you God and Thank you so much for all you do for us.

Chapter II

Based on a True Story
in a Blue mind

Jewel 25: Many have only themselves fooled, and not even close to convincing their family and friends that they have changed. Unless you have calculated steps to achieve your goals and dreams to show, no one will see your expectations nor take you seriously. Those who leave prison in such a way, without calculated steps and a divine change of heart; rush back to society to their own destruction.

(; 4 Me :)

Don't cry baby you know God has a smile behind your tears
Through the years of going through so much heartache and pain
Don't sigh baby, you know Allah will come to claim your fears
It appears that some things only the good Lord can explain
Though it remains to be seen, for the time being smile 4 me :)
Even into the drizzling rain a dreary scene still smile 4 me ;)
O.K let me spill the beans; life is but a distant dream
Don't fill the stream with more water from depths of solitary
To run downhill into the gorge of sorrow, a hopeless ravine
Jehovah will deliver from a woeful way, suffering is temporary
Despairingly as it may seem, gone ahead and smile 4 me now :)
Solace will show her overwhelming face so smile 4 me ;)
Excruciating hurt and afflictions will recede and rise
Dry your eyez baby don't cry where's that pretty little smile
(; 4 Me :)

Beautiful Moor

I'm a beautiful Moor, to the out skirts of my shore
To the deep dark inner core where it's still nice and warm
Born in the richness of time, the clime was elegant
Big and husky strong elephant in the living room
What will be on my tomb is he was much like all of us
My Ivory tusk was especially made just for my concrete wilderness
Orange Ocean spray tropic sky to look upon is 2 die 4
4 ever a Beautiful Moor, till my heart beats no more
Roar like a jungle lion when the earth opens for me
Swallow me up as the deep blue sea, no matter if I swim
Right at the rim, where life bubble up to the brim
It troubles many of them that look for life over yonder
While I'm screaming over here, yet I'm steady going under
Thunderstorms, hail, and wind block out my raging turmoil
The irony is when in the calm or rich soil, I'm unseen
Conflicting scenes make on lookers afraid to directly act
Black as oil, Berber face to trace through time
Yet shine as a glowy moon off the radiant light
That might blind, so no one looks at the beautiful Moor
My spirits soar like hungry sea gulls on a beach
Ever in reach so don't dread for the dead
Remember the secrets said in a "Beautiful Moor".

Car Seat Secretz

The hunt is on and in the night she became his prey
It wasn't easy as she was cunning and coy in her own way
Sweet talks and insinuations of what would be done given the chance
They started going to shot houses, and juke
joints bars to steal away a dance
Or to sit outside of the Arab store and drank beer
With a couple of mutual friends after work, just to be near
Here he is trying all the tricks of the trade, in order to get laid
But all those games she had already played,
she wouldn't easily persuade
She was not afraid as she soon would ride him around in her car
And she had a man that stayed close, and his family wasn't far
At the bar ordering drinks, looking enchanted, into each other eyes
He even met her boyfriend, being introduced to him, he didn't realize
What lies were beneath this conversation
disguised, they had in the open
They all set to the bar, looking slyly speaking
in code, so thought provoking
Then just like the predator knew one day his chase would give in
It had been over a year of this cat and mouse chasing
Then one night on the ride home from drinking from the store
She pulled over wanting to talk in a secluded area some more
His thoughts ran wild for sure this would be the perfect time
He walked up to her with one thing in mind, kissing from behind
No more talk leaned upside the car from the hood she felt the heat
He touched her in all the right places, on
the side of this secluded street
But this would continue in the car seat for many, many, more weeks
Till they got into a hotel to stretch out from the car seat secrets

Careered Out

How can a man get 15 years and be elated he did
Escaping the fate of an elbow, got him grinning like a kid
He said he could do it on his head, it was nuttin
About time he hit the yard he'll have 14 months in
Drug program will knock a year off, plus good time
About time you add the half-way house up, the whole nine
He says he may do 10 to 11 and 65% might come
Maybe parole and extra good time might knock off some
What about the crack law I wonder do it apply 2 me
Jail house lawyers taking books, building hopes of being free
The 1st 5 years will be spent working out, and handball
Not interested in pen pals, VI or making collect calls
Then it's time to ride closer home points drop to a low
That's about 7-8 years gone by before you know
Now it's time to program, get a GED, and go to church
Get wrapped up in becoming a better man,
save me some money from work
Cause the bidis almost over, time to check the date
Start to sale accumulated items and give away some as he anticipate
Start sending books home that's been read through the years
Walk the track, chop it up, and take flicks with peers
Envision a day of being out the feds from this conspiracy
Yet it's nothing you could ever imagine till you get 2 see

Discourses of me leaving

As I move forward toward a gleaming bright light
And pulled away from an extremely dark night
I won't fight; I'll face my fears and let it happen
And look deep in the eyez of this unknown that I've been attracting
And hear it say; you have fears of losing me now that's sick
When I thought we were growing closer, I must have dreamed it
Now I'm saying I'm out till I'm gone
Even though I don't want to die alone in this twilight zone
Like when I was born, I never wanted to leave, I was forced to go
I couldn't have turned around after the water broke
My mom glo pushed me out her womb and I came through
Goddamned my way I couldn't have gone back even if I wanted to
If I had only knew it would be like this
From the longest 5 minutes of my life to I never got over this bid.
Life is funny in the beginning then sometimes end tragic to die
So my discourses to you all are laugh now
causes you're promised to cry.

Gazing Blindly at Ebony

To have loved for one moment can be enough to last a life time
Even when it's blind, in the depths of innocence one might fine
A phone line all night conversation you hang up first no hang up last
Till the sun comes up and he's on the other end sleep, time pass
No need 2 ask, she's Ebony complexion skin, beauty of youth within
A blind phone date set up begin this relationship through a friend
He would extend his self to become his best to impress
Family begin to see him hanging around, his 1st love became obsessed
Brown sugar and caramel with chocolates
can't compare 2 her sweet face
At a fast pace they fell in love, in a lover lane begin to race
Time 2 convert the phone conversations to in person, moment defined
Exposing each other to change everything but each other mind
They met and became stuck on each other from the first touch
Chemistry make up drawn them to one
another bone 2 bone gut 2 gut
Sneaking into her room getting caught is what young lovers do
However they never had sex, just the thrill 4 him to pursue
She was afraid 2 get pregnant so often he would masturbate
And exotically play with each other but
for intercourse he'll have 2 wait
So he finally got weak and got with other women to fulfill his joy
He exposed guilty pleasure till everyone
knew and no longer could annoy
So with all his outrageous lies he got caught up not according 2 plan
Then she grew out of her fantasy and had sex with another man

Hey Heyy Heyyy

Hey heyy heyyy! I an't coming back, I'm almost free
Hey talking to you Hey Hey, who do he
think he's talking to, can't be me
He'll have to catch me, plus my name isn't hey heyy
I'm talking to you yeah you, up ahead walking all fast
Well that's everybody in front so he can kiss my a#@
You better talk to me like a grown man, plus who are you yelling at
He can't be talking to me, so I an't coming back
Hey heyy you, ok I'll turn partially around and cut my eye
Stop right now, you might as well be talking to the sky
Ohh what you jogging now, I hear feet step like horses
How do I suppose to know whose behind me with all those voices?
Hey Hey Heyy Heyyy Heyyy
If you gonna holla like you don't got no sense
You better be prepared to pay the consequence
I'll play hard of hearing and incoherent if you call that way
Hey Heyy Heyyy

In the Darkest Night

This is a place where nothing ever change in the blink of an eye
In the moments where you thought you saw
something in the blackest sky
The nights are heavy, and thick with gloom
that allows nothing 2 appear
And even when the shadows of shadows rush off still it's nothing here
But there's a conscience voice that cries out in the heaping silence
That loaded on any ear to hear except yours bringing balance
Because the voice is heavy and it asks where is everything at?
Yet not sun, moon, or stars, just cold weariness and pitch black
This place where nothing resides, no matter
how many times you blink your eye
There may be moments where you swear 2 God it was right there
It was standing right there, black as sackcloth mourners veil, dark
As brimstone coals out of hell, feeling
through brail and hearing voices
Wail, and moan, and cry and then it seems someone calls your
Name. Silence is once more heaped on you again with no
Visible image, no scenery, only the never ending landscape
Of darkness and deep. Not like in ones sleep,
but right on the edge of night terrors
Don't peep, it's the scene of one without vision,
yet he act, and has lost his way fumbling
Around in the black.
To have a vision and don't act is a daydream,
to act without vision is a nightmare

Dedicated to Melissa

Knocking on the Devil's Door

Marvin's Music hath charms, and Donte's hell hath no fury
I'm picking up the bombshell that's closest near me
Things aren't always what they appear to be
Clearly, I'm about to no doubt pay with my life dearly
You young tender thing, I desire your body so badly
Do you have a condom is what she failed to ask me
My thoughts are, she had one, and she has
only lubrication I must continue
Fulfilling my sensation of hells revelation while in you
In the car parked in the dark, flames spark like a dragging muffler
Inside her everything is touched in the raw while clutching her
Forgive me for cursing, but this explosion got me burning
She said she didn't have nothing, no protection, and no return in
If you knock on the devils door long enough
one day someone will answer
Gonorrhea came glad Aids didn't show and eat me up like cancer
I'm liken unto the man that escaped the bear being ate
To go home and stretch out on the couch and get bit by the snake
Ouch! I relate this to while I'm over my girl mate house Melissa
Last I seen her, I want forget, before she drove off I kissed her
My brother and sisters it's time to bail we keep looking a better way
Guns I'm trying to sale, my mind tells me
stop or its jail, but I want obey
Things I thought was good for me I found out obviously weren't
I took fire into my bosom and later found out I got burnt
I'm in prison living off reckless decisions hard lessons got learnt
Picture me outside knocking and yelling to open up till the
Devils door knob got turnt

Memoirs of a Gothic Society

The modern day dark age of European Medieval times are upon us
We're a strange looking motely bunch,
with tattoos and body piercings
African women lip plates, don't have nothing
on Native women 12 gauge ears
Eyez blacken as soot with ink to appear
more devilish with silver horns
Ohh what sharp fangs you have grandma,
the granddaughter notice fangs
The grandmother had since she was no older than seventeen
Now in old age looking quite the character,
betcha didn't see this coming
Scarification rigid on the backs of Gothic
men that claim 2 be reptilians
Slithering around this hell bound society has many cults frighten
They said we're gone too far into this madding dark and lost our way
All black leather on with the music blasting
chanting something murky
The Artist sings, I'm in this nightmare of dreams 2 not be redeemed
(I'm a sinner)
If despair reigns supreme in this blind land one eye reign king
Demons scream- I'm a sinner
Preachers says lord be with you son and his upper lips quivers and say
With a smirk smile, the lord, who is the lord? Screw the Lord
I'm hopeless bound of the taboo of India pain be upon me
None will ever see the sorrow I see in this Godforsaken society.

Marvin Thomas

Midnight Lust

He's a long ways from home, the nights about gone and he's not done.
Still alone, he's roamed around looking companionship since sunset
What could one get hours after midnight,
nothing decent only cheap tricks?
It's getting to late can't be picky or choosey,
he needs something real quick
You know where any girls at he ask as he pulls up on the hooker block
Its way after 12 o'clock and its a few folks
out standing in the parking lot
Someone yells have you checked down to the Red Carpet Inn
You'll see a girl walking back and forth with sex cheap as sin
He hurries quickly trying to catch her before someone else.
First stop is an all-night convenient store for
condoms, one must protect themselves.
Then he rushes on in his lust hoping she's not gone
Ohh yeah with a big smile he say what do
we have here as he comes up on
A pretty young girl not knowing she's an undercover police officer
Well you can guess the rest.

No Title

Stars, Moons, Quasars, and constellations
guides a nation, my revelation
Our destination, when we arrive to stay alive only to thrive in misery
Or is it me, to see the only lonely faint hearted and the dear departed
Forgive me cause this here is real, to reveal how we kill each other
Father, Mother, Sister, and Brother smother
out our nieces and nephews
We all lose, if one lose we must choose one, but we're all confused.
So we destroy a whole nation to prove a point what do he or she want
We all want power, erect towers, then die violent, remain silent 4ever
Well at least for years, an ocean of tears, we've cried when they've died
But what good is inside my soul, my spirit, my tender heart wonders
As it rain down hail and lighting and thunder
and was cast under a bridge
To hide from the pain the hurt, the love, the bliss, is it your first time
Your mind, your strength, your passion, all that kindle the fire of joy
Out the best of times, the worst of times, a
title of our situation whichever one.

PERFECT LOVE STORY

He was miserable without her, as she nestled inside his arms.
She held on to his heart for dear life, knowing she has it all.
Neither would let go for a moment, which closes the door on love.
Neither could go on as they lived life like they once did before.
Who could endure the thought of losing such a one?
Only confusion and pain would answer that question.
All I know is there is nothing outside of their love that matters.
That was strong enough to possible get in the way of each other.
And as time moved on the days to months to years,
So did they continue and did what God had set out for them.
Conformed, and transformed them into each other cut perfectly.
As grooves were notched out into each other lives set adorably.
Loving each other for life is the ending of a perfect love story.

Dedicated to my loved ones

Reaching Back Across

As I open up and show you more of who Marvin is
I can't help but think how much easier it's become as time wiz by
We've come so far and tried so hard 2 connect, we must keep trying
Undying commitment and dedication is what we need 2 carry on
Searching relentlessly in the deep uttermost parts of ourselves 2 help
Our unborn through this storm that hasn't even took form yet
I'll never, never, never, never, never quit,
I'm on the other side doing mine
Fear not, 2 explore beyond the deep horizons of the days of our lives
In the richness of our youth we're thriving,
in the end so much done in vain
All you have is your name; make it and your
children, children's great with fame
I was prescribed 70 months of lethal pain; I'll share it with you
Imagine me rough around the edges, now
have elegance you can make it too
Financial Health is serious as a heartbeat;
separate the weak from the elite
The prison cell I'd lived in was 25,920 lbs. of pressure all around
It turned me into a diamond, no more a black coal worthless
Now I'm bound to dazzle, sparkle, and shine the light on the people
Diamonds are 4ever so know I'll always brighten the way no matter
Where you stay! What time of Day!

Republican's Cry

1854 Horace Greeley from the New York Tribune
An editor set an elaborate scheme on the world stage
A diabolical mind on literary platforms seduce politics
Suggested to the Red Men Whig party, as formally known
Long are the days gone to be Red, but it's time to be white
And the Whig party would become known as the republican's
So Abraham Lincoln would be 1st to hold this office
To relinquish powers from the south, to free the slaves
The 16th president wasn't afraid to sign the
emancipation proclamation
Under the republicans watch, they felt it was time to seize power
But when will it end, ohh my God when will it stop
Republican's Cry smaller government, less spending and no tax
With condescending motives, these elephants future looks bleak
No (GOP) Grand Old Party can see 14 trillion dollars deficits
Ohh how they wail, don't cry now you help did this
No Republican has no clear vision for the country they love
Yet their #1 objective in 2012 is to beat Obama
The Democrats produced Obama Care can't wait 2 get it
Sorry you guys was late to the punch, maybe next time
Don't cry now, looking all crazy, ohh how they wail

Dedicated to Luke the Physician
10:19

Serpents and Scorpions

Behold I give unto you power to tread on serpents
and scorpions and over all the powers of the enemy;
and nothing shall by any means hurt you.

I alert you that threats are all around, be under no illusion
So much confusion between what's safe and what's deathly living
Life is fragile given so either in fear we walk or bravely live
Or give into fear that reeks on you and get your life over took
Don't look directly into their biddy eyes,
just move cautiously and wise
They thrive on worry so don't hurry across ridged enemy lines
Cause you can't find the object of your search with tall grass
Get pecked in the a#@ or a sting in your personal private thing
Coming to you as the woman of your dreams or an ace bone cone
Then all of a sudden boom! Bethcha didn't see that coming
Burned by my woman, set on fire blinded by the fury of frantic lust
Who can I trust, My best friend is all I can depend on
But when he's gone, she's gone, I'm left alone to suspect
The peck and constant sting comes from the same extreme frie-enemy
When we see the warning signs remember the spiritual divine
Has gave us power to outshine any darkness that appear
And make our way clear without any dangers or hurt
Ohh what evil lurk in the thistle, brushes, and thicket of the bush.

Spectacular Mistakes

Spectacular mistakes I made, I'm afraid I paid for them dearly
Even though you know I didn't mean to do it, I'm so sincerely "sorry"
On starry nights I gaze up ask God 2 forgive me "sorry"
Causing family heartache and pain when I'm in error
Hard lessons learned made a hard bed get turned into terror
Let me share the experience that has defined my relevance
It don't make sense to fall into silly peer pressure
If they call you'll come, if you fail the test police arrest ya!
Whatever my wants, I don't mix them with my needs
Greed always has its way of rearing its ugly head
Instead of further telling lies to cover up my mistakes
Owning up to them is taking responsibility it's what it takes
DWI's I had since I like to drive and drink, it makes me think
I really must love to walk or put innocent lives in danger
Protection from the stranger means laws has its reason
This leaves me to believe what one does affect everyone else
Either you do what's right for self or you'll have no friends left
And you'll ask a question that you know the answer all along
It's not the mistake we make, but what we
do after to correct the wrong

Inspired by Michelle Jenkins

Strange Sexual Encounters of an Intense Kind

Neither the man nor woman could wait as he was on his way
He was headed to her trailer and she watched out the window waiting
They both were in different relationships, but
somehow bumped into each other
Strangely enough chemistry collided, and
they both fell for one another
Coming into paradise and as the door
opened they collapsed to the floor
Intensely on each other on the dirty rug where the pet dog pooped
Her kids just happen to be over grandmother's
house what a coincidence
Guilty consciences were buried underneath
her bosom drawn by his chest
Sexual attraction is madding and left
unattendent can cause carpet friction
Welcomed addiction of pleasurable pains
rubbing together like two nickels

Kissing as he has never kissed before and
her hormones rage out of control
Rolling on the floor relentlessly, wildly, like a crocodile and it's pray
Her man will be home soon, and his woman
will worry of him coming home
Both probably calling around the same time, right now both are gone
Sweating, panting, yearning, moaning and
stinging in a lot of mischief
Their pores gush attraction in vibes and
gyration of endless deprived senses
Touching, caresses, holding, and invading
the forbidden body of one another
Nothing is left sacred among their significant
other as they lie on the floor
Tired, bruised, and satisfied laughing into
each other hazel and blue eyes

Dedicated to Ayyub Cornelius
Aka. IU

The Forest and the Tree

As far as I can see, I can't see the forest from the tree
So If I had only six months to tell it, this is what it wood be
If I had six great big long months to pursue happiness b4 I go
I wood first let you know, how I seen trees strip
down, and skinny dip in the icy cold
In a 40 below froze sea temperature as the winter snow
Till spring comes sunny heat, they'll wrap back up with leaves
That wood cover like cloths taking every moment to breathe
As forest as I wood see, wood be beautiful smiles and bright faces
I'll reflect from my youth as a young whipper
snapper in my limbs running warm sap
Anxious to shoot up as a tree of heaven and
reside where jay bird wings flap
To have a limited time to bear fruit only
makes us understand a season
That roots extends from the tree of knowledge
and trees of life in the African region
So I'm not evergreen, but ever changing
this steam with every heartbeat
In this wildlife wilderness cut down and beat to
a pulp is the unstoppable end I'll reach
I wood see in slow motion me stand as an oak by the ocean
Anticipating the moment I wood leave
Branch out into another place coming in naked from the icy seas
So while six months quickly leaks out of the top of the hour glass
I must now live everyday as the continuation of the last

The Great Recession 2007

When I first heard of the feds, this is what they said.
They had something like king size beds
and it was better than the state.
You ate great; you would at times have T-bone
steak, or on your plate lobster tail.
A cellphone to call home and you get to relate to
all types of celebrities while you're gone.
Ohh was they wrong during 07 the recession that hit great
I got caught up in a crime that sent me beyond state without weights.
The feds got me they didn't feed good, biscuits were hard as wood
No celebrities just lying Negros from the
hood, shaking hands and hugging
Where the golf courses at, where's Wesley Snipes, T.I and Mike Vick.
For all we know Burney Madoff is being secretly held in N.C
Ohh look there's Petey Pablo and we all broke in this great recession.
Like the Great Depression, but it's still card tables in the block
Store man got a shop with roll up cigarettes and a cap of weed
Ohh how the streets bleed that's why we're
piled up three bunk beds high.
And so many waiting to get in through the
gates, my fate was I fell on hard times,
In 2007 when the recession was great.
Hanging with the wrong crowd found my-
self with guns in my possession.
Going along with the program wasn't cutting
it when others are in confession
So it's time to go away for a while during
the time of the great recession

Chapter III

The Evolution of a Poet

Jewel 125: There is a thin line between a genius and insanity. It is so thin that to look at it up close will blur your vision.

1976 Prince of Darkness

Letters are scribbled in the dark, only a
sparked imagination lights the way
Words form as buds unfold before the coming forth of day
The greatest story 4ever told on my soul and it's for sale
Look no further if you search for Lucifer in this living hell
Deep rooted within yourselves you'll find no pitch fork or pointy tail
Evil men do is the devil within you, or goodness
is God and the stronger will prevail
Drink with me what you thought was holy
water, might be a shot of red wine
Then let's define what you think divine reality
is, that's all in your righteous mind
Brace yourself in the face of death face your worst fears
Then stagger forward in the tunnel of eternal light that's 4ever clear
This will make you teary eyed at comic, and
burst out and laugh at the tragic
With a smirk say goodness of the world is sorcery and black magic
Cause the desecration of the pulpit, preacher
tell the truth wrapped in lies
Ahh Hehh screaming God dammed our ways
to hell with proof Heaven our prize
I prefer the land of Kush, with dried olives
leaves rolled up in Bible paper
Hearing voices from this burning brush whispering
if not you then who will save you
Dame, sure ant' the Pope leaders that fondle and
squeeze that nature out lil alter boyz
Or nuns that want give you none less you're a
sister with rosemary beads used as sex toys
So I ask self where are you going and self say, God don't thou know
To and Fro in the earth 2 kill something, self is our strongest foe
No more discussion, end of story period . . .

Dedicated to the women in this Poem

BLACK BEAUTY

Ebony was the pecan shell that held Michelle Obama
A woman of German dark rich chocolate is fascinating
Kelly Roland mahogany style features was stunning
Jet Black beauty as glamorous as Oprah Winfrey
Almond brown Jada Pinkett-Smith is a joy to watch
God's greatest creation of a deep rich mocha color
Was Gloria Thomas with a gorgeous walnut tint blended?
Cappuccino shade made Beyoncé Knowles a superstar
A woman African roots shows in her dark brown eyez
So exotic and foreign than anything eyez ever seen
The heritage of caramel outer veils has strength and life
Maya Angelou secret to black beauty was phenomenally astonishing
Carrying the ethnic essences in the brown genes
The Moorish woman has immense wealth of petroleum oil

Coffee and Lonely Moments

As I rolled over to awake
You were on my mind
Even before the time to make coffee
You were still very close behind
I turned to look
But to my disappointment
You were not yet there
Though I know with God's Love
Grace and Mercy, every precious
Moment soon we will share
And so I stare in my bed
On the other side
Thinking about my love
Coming to give me a ride
Yet at moments it seems
You're with me all along
Cause your presence God
Graced me with, is so divinely strong.

Distant Traveler

In the deep corners of my mind, I find that I'm safe and warm.
Closing my eyes is pulling down the blinds,
got me feeling right at home
As my mind recline on the lazy-boy of my thoughts
Then drift off and reminisce, strolling down
memory lane, a peaceful walk
This is a place of rest for the ever weary on this dreary path
Cozy memories in the darkness, like stepping bare- footed in the grass
On my travels I unravel the comforts that I seldom have
And cherish the moments like this relaxing in bliss without a mask
People come through and greet me frequently,
think they are my friend
Unfortunately I have to distance myself
because of all the stink they in
So when they ask where I've been, I send word, I'm on a dusty road
With men that find rest in luxurious beds beside a Kohler commode
Who travel to Burger King on Wednesday and Tuesday its KFC?
Pass time Square to their residency; rub their bellies fall back to sleep
This just isn't me, you may see me stopped and off I stare
It's like checking in my bedroom, and I'm not there
I'm on a highway traveling and smiling with family, I'm gone
Through windows of my imaginative soul, I behold home.

Dr. King

When he was 8 years old Micheal "Luther King Jr" was his name
Dying wishes from his grandfather got it all changed
Now he's known as Dr. Martin Luther King Jr.
He realized that being racist would ruin you
With all the racist things he had seen as a teen he had a dream
While the south was in turmoil, burning, churches and human beings
So as the cross burned in his yard he stayed with God
He earned a Doctors degree, but it didn't change his façade
The plot grows thicker for soon this man will get shot
For now he tied the knot with Ms. Coretta Scott
Whites set in front of the bus, In the back is just us
Dr. King started to march in a civil rights movement
A non- violence peaceful movement, seeking to turn the other cheek
But Cops beat and slaughtered us like field cattle
Flooding us in battle with firefighters water hoses stinging
Now it's just racist looks where there was a sting
We finally did reached the mountain top out of Kings' Dream

Generation X

From the time I was a filthy little kid to now
I could never tell you all the amazing things I did
No way, No how, those secrets went to the grave with me
So don't try to pick my brains or plot schemes to trick me
Get me out my info, somethings are left better off not 2 know
It could cause a ripple effect in the pool of reality check
Blow your mind, then all the time say he's probably lying.
Well keep trying and maybe I'll give you a clue to guess
The test of life is weird, like the twilight zone
Duna Nuna Duna Nuna close your eyes when you've seen too much
The shores of time bleed secrets, the bloody moon shine
Revealing the future yet to be killed, the whole ocean filled
Blood spill was promised to my Generation X fate sealed
Revelation speaks of a red sea, and the dead would walk;
The earth among us, well this is what they in darkness said
Follow me into the wise from the wicked ways
In the last dayz sacrifice in life must be made
Don't be afraid to give up your life for this is your purpose
Many will come, but I don't believe it, He's the one
Is what they say when it's all said and done, hurry up run
What is he doing, he's beginning to believe in himself
Even in death inside the things he tried to hide will come forward
And the people will say finally I see him, Man that's Awesome.

Inspiration

My 8th grade teacher, Mrs. Annie Gainer, said I could be what I will
Once I acquired a certain skill, nothing could ever hold me back
Even though I act wild she said strikes of
being black must make me think
She pushed confidence on me, and told me
mistakes are a part of being a man
I ran with that, not fully understanding then, but I know now
How could I put my family and myself through so much turmoil?
The spoils of war are my restitution fines, it's a
war going on and I'm stuck in the middle
Riddle me this, what man pursues the
failures in life hoping to achieve
Mrs. Gainer got me by myself and kept it so real
And talked to me, and made me feel like her son

Message in a Bottle

I wish to be with you in person, but unfortunately I can't
These frail bodies don't last long and barley get us through 70 years
It appears I'll have to be with you in thought
and mind, and leave behind
This message that's escaped through the depth of time to you
I find a great people born blind and not knowing what to do
Marcus Garvey, said awake you sleepy giants
and accomplish what you will
Marvin Thomas, said he who can't think can't survive, now that's real
We must live and pass down to our seed what they need to achieve
Instead we bleed for what greed, that was left, we must believe
Not having enough cash to put away the
deceased and passed in the earth
Forefathers blast through money not even learning a dollars worth
Even at birth, our babies are not planned, they're mostly mistakes
It takes a stable income to raise a baby and make it great
Noble Drew Ali said I am not going to wake up all the Asiatic
(At once). Because they may tear up something we're such fanatics
The resonance of our self-destruction has come to the for front
Who's willing to die with me so our children can get what they want
Our beautiful babies are in homes with crazies and the foolish
When the parents finally awake sometime it's too late for rulership
The child is wild, out of control, and following down the same road
In efforts to save them now will definitely take it's toll
Raise our soul from this dark state of mind and begin to follow
This is my God word to awake the conscience mind
from the other side of the shores of time
Message in a Bottle

No, Not like This

God please help me, the forces of nature has proclaimed me enemy
So I move on through the ethers with a heavy chip on my shoulder
Don't feel sorry 4 me, feel sorry 4 yourself for what's in store 4 me
That is going over my highest height and
attaining to my depths even lower
But you may be wasting precious time in a life that's slipping away
And those opposed against me have declared war; it's the test of time
Elements of the earth ripping my body apart in the form of decay
God why you allow me to get way over
here while others are left behind
No need 4 crying I got a job to do might as well get to it
I feel I'll suffer pain but this comes at the price of growth
The young ones need to see me be a man so they can do it
As they research me and see how I acted and what I did up close
Take care of your family, love mama, no
matter what, and respect yourself
If your dad hasn't left, then love him too, till light shine on you
Do all you can son while you live, because the light is death?
Truth is we're not all going to make it, but we hate what's true
Don't be afraid of what you might find down there amongst misery
You must stay within reach of the people so you can aid and assist
No matter what you see, persist to finish the work of destiny
But don't leave a life incomplete, so say God please not like this
No God not like this, to perish without having all my work done
Allow me 2 continue on, No not like this

Poor Sinner

During my time, our men would breed
with their women like roaches.
Then leave them to fend for themselves while they got ghost.
If you got close to the project walls you could hear single mama's say.
To their nappy headed boys, you make me
sick; you're just like your daddy.
Why did I act that way, how did I get like
this, my life as a poor sinner?
In an age, where whole generations came up
relating to being chronically broke
Picking up bad habits like drinking and smoking
in our room while mama struggle at work.
We ducking school, cause cool school cloths
haven't been mama's top priority.
And all the pre-cooked oven baked food in the
freezer seems way more appealing.
Ohh what a feeling, hanging with the OG's
schooling us how to get our cash up
Either way I'm stuck in a poverty stricken
community living day to day
Shameless to say welfare block cheese, and
Salvation Army cloths maybe the way
Pray for me, the lost poor sinner.

Dedicated to 7 out of 10 in prison

Shhussssh

He's shown no consistency in nothing except yelling deal me in
To the poker table house man every time the games begin
And then walk fast past the GED class to the rec yard
No disregard to completing what many years ago he started
He says it's too hard, but that's anything that's worth having
Dropping out of school and quitting jobs has become his pattern
He's to every social gathering homies put together to entertain
Every music video BET show he knows its name, always the same
Everyday bobbing his head rapping the words all crazy loud
While playing chess or dominos trying to sing over the crowd
Every word that comes out is unarticulated, broken English or curse
Overheard he got kids but when he come home its women first
His thirst for drugs and alcohol seeps out in his conversation
You preach the book of revelation; he says it's not in his equation
Someone ask what will he do for a living once being released
With his pants sagging and corn rolls at 50 years old at least.
Shhussssh I want to laugh too. But I'm in my cell doing this
What foolish pleasures we miss, I'm in meetings teaching his;
Story and it's no mystery why they come
back to prison for another bid
Tell me you going out to start a business, I'll pucker my lips up and
Say Shhussssh

Inspired by the month of March

Sleepless Endless Nightz

Little Cherokee Native American girl you scalped my heart
You came in like men in gone with the wind then tore me apart
With your tomahawk eyes that has scared me, plagues me daily
Can't get rid of promises you made of us at a POW wow lately
My dreams catcher can't catch no dreams if I can't get no sleep
I pound my pillow to make it as comfortable as it can be
Feathers dangle loose like the tattoo you have Cherokee Indian girl
Though you'll say you're not Indian, You vanished in the spirit world
Man I can't sleep; it's the month of March when we both met
The month that sparked this fiery voice in me, I'll never forget
Where are you, I ask wide awoke, probably on some reservation
A place reserved only for you to stay with strict federal regulation
Me on the other hand, I'm cast out to the raving wolves
To be eaten alive by black bears in the woods, stomped by pig's hooves
Tossing and turning, burning and yearning to see your face
Yanked form your life like a power cord, longing the outlet embrace
It's spring again and life begins with the end nowhere in sight
So I'll continue to search the stars in these sleepless endless Nightz

Solace of Gloria

Weeping 4 her son who didn't come home last night
Left in a fright not knowing if 4 good he's gone
When will that phone call come in that'll make her cry?
Saying your son has been found dead in a ditch, try 2 remain calm
The storm is over now, nothing else 2 be afraid of
God love would have him in this gloomy dark dreary day
Let's pray together and know all will work itself out
Her son hasn't called yet and she's about worried crazy
No consideration, no thoughtfulness of what he does
Out drinking and chasing women maybe even on drugs
Ambulances and police cars squeal by make her jumpy
It's something about prayer that really changes things
The stings of life lumps up in her throat to draw a tear
Stirred up as a nervous wreck till the doorbell rings
It's her son dragging in with cloths on from the other day
Eyez flame red, face sunk in and she utters these words
Boy! You nun got poe and lapsed as a race horse
Running the road like a stray dog all night gone crazy
Her baby goes flop face 1st on the bed hung over
Then God whispered "Gloria one day he'll get sober and see".
So find solace in me as he writes your name in the sands of time

It is the most precious thing in the world to help someone achieve their goals and dreams and this is something that I want to do through my poetry. As I create the proses of these wonderful events that tell more than a story, it is my deepest aim and gift to share my life with those willing to read and see what parts relate to their very own and what might seem familiar in the life of someone else. I have been to the bottom of the valley and have risen to the mountain top. While the early parts of my life had peculiar turn of events. From a life style of growing up in a small town just wanting to be someone known for helping someone turned into a nightmare of trying to escape from around everyone I knew. I left my small town roots with the adventures of having a job at a chicken plant called Perdue Farms, and meeting and marrying my wife for the next 7 years. This was somehow short lived because not only was she 25years older than me but she lost her drive and hustle to achieve her goals through hard work and wanted to depend on a staggering government social system to help her the rest of the way out. So after a few months of figuring out that this was not who I suppose to grow old with, I reacquainted myself with a friend of the family that I had met on my ex-wife side. As at the time she was married and so was I, so no lines were crossed but now that I was divorced and she was; it seemed like a perfect fit so we begin to date and shortly after got married. It was all a fantasy because outside of the physical attraction, we really had nothing else to hold us together. It was meant only for a time and she was in the purpose to prepare me for the woman that I'm with now. I've been married for two years now and happier than I've been in both of my prior relationships combined. I've overcome the sickness of failure which tells us who have made a mistake to give up, why keep trying when all everyone wants to do is judge us. I've overcome extreme poverty of living from house to house and all your cloths are in a bag. Picking up cans for extra change, and sleeping in abandon buildings with a trackfone. The impossible decisions that we make rather good or bad we must be held accountable for them.

The Weak versus The Elite

The strong feed off the weak and peep at them as lunch meat
Off the weak backs, nations are built and economic wealth is reached
Can anyone teach weak minds to become strong and not follow along
Carried on by any wind of doctrine, not
even knowing they're dead wrong
It's the fearless, upright, and independent
who represent that entire nation
That's how the Elites do; someone has to
guide those with misinformation
What do weaklings really own that can't be crept in and took away
To their dismay they think their strong till its 2 late and they fall prey
Without power and wealth a man is made
to suffer, but knowledge is key
Weakness lie naked in ever man except he reckon with his infirmities
This power is information that is crucial and is demanded by the Elite
The more advance move as a constant
heartbeat, the weak is always sleep
The weak make excuses and pass the blame when it don't go their way
They pay for mistakes that was passed down
to them with nothing 2 say
The weak will never reach their full
potential, their peak is utter defeat
It's pitiful how the Elite devour the weak like the wolf and the sheep
Weak think close surroundings while the Elite
think international and the world
Elite make laws that they know men will
break so they can take their girl
They also control the money cause without
finance man has no woman
And without the woman the man falls weak
and into destructions he runs in.

Chapter IV

4 The true few that knew me.

Jewel 137: One must become superior to their environment and find equilibrium among their peers; by doing this all the obstacles that surround them will become stepping stones for achieving success, and peers will move along beside you in formation/

African American

In the land of the free home of the brave
We 1ˢᵗ came in as a slave, slave master beat us crazy
Now we lounge around and call ourselves nigger
But I'm trying to figure what triggered this insanity
It's almost like using profanity when it comes to this
What generosity we showed when owner's came in
And raped our women we stood with water in our eyez
Then if Willie didn't kill us he left only our lives
Families dignity gone, men lost honor and found a coward
We use to hunt lions, rule cities with a staff and shield
Now in a cotton field we fight amongst each other
Call our brother Uncle Tom because he reside in the house
Along with your spouse, and the master doing whatever
Negro please you better get your mind right
We're on a prison plantation now doing the same thing
The dream of freedom comes with a sting of truth
For it we must die, get sacrificed or slaughtered
A martyr for the cause of African American is we
Africa has many nations, have we discovered our roots
We're off shoots from a distant land such a beat up man
Shaken and disturbed because of all the terror we seen
A land irrigated on blood, cause our dreams to be scary.

Dedicated to my other mother Sheilena Little

Black Roses

I loved Brien like my own flesh and blood
Despite poverty how it drug us through the mud
Both of us two was from the same bud
We tried to come up when society called us thugs
We dug our own pit and we had to sleep in it
Buried with the weeds we were just tinny tiny seeds
The both of us had needs ready to rise above top soil
Having to overcome rock and gravel, chaos and turmoil
We press on this thorny path, we were so green
Didn't know the places we wish to go was a distant dream
Sheilena and Gloria jean my mama's cut from the same vines
Both assured me after my time would be there when I leave
Fresh fragrance I breath when the sun shine on us again
Life extended from two roses, so we can unfold in the end
Him and I will reach the mountaintop as
Martin Luther King and Moses
Sheilena was one of the few who knew my true depth
And witness my growth to the heights of heaven step by step
Brien let me moved in and this began a lifetime of more than friends
As we moved in the sin got caught up till the unpredictable end
All I know is through tough times, true
family was present at my lowest
So as I rise and come up, I must give back to my black roses

Concrete Jungle

Monkey noises of intense levels resonate all over the common area
Screaming at the top of their lungs and his dawg standing beside him
You see that? Ohh he's a beast as he scores, yelling at the game
So much obscenity being used its insane and
women names abused its misogyny
Screaming on the phone at the top of their
lungs send the money or else
He'll have her touched and his kids is in dire need of the basic
I'm bored, I'm bored it's nothing to do, it's nothing to get into he says
Books and education is dead, his thoughts
are scathing towards correction
Then he sits quiet twiddling his thumbs wondering what comes next
Then all of a sudden, he leaps up screams
chow like a C/O to see who flinch
Bust out into laughter at a few that got up with
head phones in and then they set back down
Movie on! Then the whole jungle gets quiet as a church mouse
Early in the morning hear the roar of noise seep into the dorm
As they come back from chow stirring their shot of coffee
Who's next on the microwave in the lingering line the length of a boa?
Bowls of soup, wraps, pizzas and one holds it up by cooking a meal
Licking fingers, stirring wildly opening
and closing the microwave door
Its hell's kitchen and you may not get in until one full hour
Shower time, another line cold water is all that is left for you
Along with curly black hair on the shower stalls and dingy soap scum
Almost turned into an animal from man in this concrete jungle

ERUDITION

I enamor the art of music, musician sing with instruments with string.
Melodies conquer my soul like the moors
of Spain the peninsula of Arabia.
Herbie Hancock and Miles Davis bring
blues deep as the Atlantic Oceans.
Jazz that clash with the spirit and makes for a thriving lively heart,
That race more than Vietnam victims
screaming at the end of his world.
On to the next red seas, olive gardens, and white lightning burst.
Ohh! How the stars, moon, planets, and quasars intrigue me.
So exquisitely constructed look up at beauty in all its glory.
Profusely trying to search the end of ages dial plates of heaven.
Imhotep was the 1st Benjamin Bannaker of this era and time
Wisdom is as eccentric to man as Cleopatra was to Caesar.
Brought forth by day on camel extravagant nights by Bentley.
Her romantic tongue of different languages arouses my mental.
Exploring the depths of myths causes creativity of a renaissance.
Making her flamingo dance more expressive and enchanting 2 watch.
Thriving inside the culture of modern day
poetry rhythms, throb like gypsies.
It's me only seeing my teeth as stated in the songs of Roland.
In this gloomy darkness so pervasive, one must be a connoisseur still.

Fair Beloved

I've just realized the most beautiful thing I've ever seen
Fair beloved, you're everything that I ever dreamed of
Her lovely eyez mean the sunrise, she winks the crescent moon
Breathtaking perfume has left a scent that's enchanting
I can't believe she touched me, now I'm so consumed
Pulchritude women are never as vibrant as you are
With all your splendor my soul bow down and surrender
Your magnificent love and eccentric affection for me
Is overwhelming, feelings of perfection you express?
Are so eclectic, her language put together and spoken
Fair Beloved she's so radiate I can't behold all of her charms
Between your legs are eternal rivers running wild around my truth
The nipples of her breast are bursting with fountains of youth
Ingredients of my happiness is the sweet taste of her
It's simply delicious, taste buds in flame of desire
I'm slowly guided into her fiery pleasures of spiritual bliss
Ravished by her devoted love, I relish her holy kiss
I can't fight the urge to deny you over powering my soul
So roll back the clouds and let me feel your tenderness
Underneath this baby blue blanket in the sky
Over laid with a navy blue view we lie, covered from the fire
I thank it might rain when I die, don't cry beloved
A love affair will pass and gone on by, but you and I will always be.
Dedicated to God and the love of my life.

House of Illusion

A prisoner sits in the solitude of his little bitty cell
And goes into his wishing well of thoughts so provocative
To write a passionate letter to the woman of his dreams
As he hoist up beams on the empty lot of a fairy tale
Really it's madness in this living hell, his imagination runs wild
In the bile's of this insane asylum he finds a loving heart
Seeing what he wants 2 see in the dark both being together
On his letter he writes when I get home have my child
He sets up dry walls of good intention, makes space for the lies
Well-spoken wise words on the phone
building beautiful conversations
Till revelation of truth seems strange reality sets in
Then writes I need you to visit baby look into windows of my eyes
That recognize the proof, no matter how far fetch or sincere
She can notice the tears and know that this here is real
Convincing her she's not in hopelessness, soon she'll wait no more
Unless she close the door of fascination and the Illusion disappears

Intellectually Blind

I'm hurt, I'm mad, I'm in love, and I'm lonely
I'm concerned about all the burdens that God lie on me
As foolish as I am, I still got sense enough to know
That it takes struggle and sacrifice to keep from being poe
I'm sad, I'm crazy, and I'm full of lots of feelings
Have I got hate in my heart for women so appealing?
It's confusing I know why I'm so wretched towards a female
Maybe it's because I can't touch her, my feelings are in hell
I'm amused, I'm baffled, and I'm seduced by misery
I'm heavy in spirit, my eyes cry so vigorously
I'm nauseous, I'm empty, and I'm not even in pain
I'm something else awful so numb, I'm so ashamed
I'm something different than I was the day before
Till the day I'm vanquished, till the day I'm no more
I'm in a world of anguish; I'm in a life of suffering
I'm in a time of joy; I'm in a body of buffeting
I'm at peace for the moment, gone from angry to feeling fine
I'm at liberty; I'm locked-up but not intellectually blind

Last of a Dying Breed

The last of a dying breed, now here is their story.
Folks helping in times of need, no need to worry.
No selfish acts, or attacks of greed, but in a hurry.
To aid and assist, ohh how I miss times like this.

A helping hand doing all they can, a close knit hood.
Community guide boy to man was understood.
It wasn't planned, but without saying and it felt good.
To keep families intact and having each other back.

People pick you up give a ride, to another side.
Through rain or its hot and dried, then feet get tired.
No good intention mask behind to hide but real abide.
No need to be afraid, no one trust ever gets betrayed.

Neighbors bring over a loaf of bread, we got the cheese.
Societies help keeping these in the deep freeze.
A deer shoulder, ham, garden peas, and collard leaves.
Days are gone, down the street people depend on.

If your car break down the road folks quick to stop.
And push you out of ongoing traffic into a parking lot.
Strangers help change tires that showed wires and then popped.
Is there any left I plead, the last of a dying breed?

Marvin's Garden

Marvin's Garden is where I breathe in my fresh scent of roses
Exposed naked pink in color velvet texture to my nose
As I open and close the leafy petal to experience
the nature of the pure natural
To unravel the budded joy and sow living waters
For this perfect flower to capture
My mouth recesatation blows on tu-lips
And revivify the senses of the pads of the lily
Until it wide open, while unbroken but free.

Missing me when I'm gone

Entry #6
Miss me when I'm gone is how I feel about friends
No one is thinking of me as I think of you
Someone we knew and we happened to part ways
Engulfed in a perfect maze, in our on perfect minds
The times past, and we get lost trying to come through
To you it may be a day dream away from the real
But how should you feel if no one cared about you
Enough to just think about you, on their mind sometime
Every now and then missing time they use to spend
That's O.K through, trust and believe, that in the end
Your eyez will leak clear fluid called a tear
No matter how sincere, it maybe when it hit
Some don't get it, give me my flowers while I live
Miss me when I'm gone is how I feel about friends
But why in the end, it's like they never was there
Vanish in thin air at the toughest of hard times
Where's my partner in crime, my ace bone coon
I can only assume that you never was real or true
So much we made it through, but now can't be found
New people held me down, that I came to knew
Now look at you, come crying talking about way back then
A so called friend with sentimentality, but in all reality
Miss me when I'm gone

Much 2 do of Nothing

Wanting to pick her up and twirl her around, lifted off the ground
To embrace her in the air stare into her sparkling eyez with joy
His face shining and glowing from the reflection of her elegance
The man heart pounds and race while his
mind run wild with anticipation
What comes next, it's more than the kiss,
the sex, but intimate conversation
Its powerful, and an explosive revelation of
how they made it to one another
Who would have known? Who would have
believed these two would hook up?
It's for this one reason he completes with urgency these task to please
His day starts to appease her every desire,
thinking what could be better
He says to himself I got to run to the corner
store to get roses and wine
Before she arrives, take the hamburger meat out the freezer for lasagna
After he's done cooking, watches his watch to run the bath water
He put the fresh scented beads in and gets massage oils to relax her
Where the candles at as he panics, whew,
ohh relieved cause he finds them
Hid them from his self, what's left what did I forget he says
As he watches his watch and peep out the door
He vacuum the floor, clean rooms, and smells of
Couture with fresh breeze in the evening
This perfect evening of many, he's dressed and soft music in the air
She's almost there as she calls on his iPhone to prepare him
He peeps out the window, and there she go, last look in the mirror
Her car door slams, and hears the keys jingle and jiggle
He rushes with exceedingly joy and happiness to greet at the door
To open it, pick her up and twirl her around, and show her
What he has in store

REVELATIONS

One day these writing will appear and someone near and dear
Will express with great admiration what do we have here
Sincerely yours but I disappeared along long time ago
But the things I revealed in my vision, I can't say I told you so
Like how the modern time sun people all of a sudden raised up
Recognized the true truth and from then no longer gazed up
Stopped depending on God outside and had a look at self
And seen the kingdom of heaven, and seen no more death
It's no more crack left, just meth heads for the other side
The jig was up that racist capitalist practice of genocide
Modern terms you probably call it now ethnical cleansing
And in this day and age corrupt minds need a good rinsing
After the brain washing, we've been badly mind freaked
Instead of with Christ the Angel, Chris Angel led the blind sheep
Don't peep, but you're about to experience some real magic
Close your eyez and open them to a world of no tragic
Just remember what I said; only the dead die
And those that live drink from living waters that never run dry

That's just the Way it was

If I'm dead broke can I be truly happy, miserable is the rich man
But rich, if I'm too cold can relocate to Florida
and when cold turn on the fan
If I'm honest all my life then die telling a lie will I be forgiven
Then will I be a day late a dollar short of
being rewarded eternal living
If I was an ugly guy how much cash would I
need to pick and choose the best girl
Then they would bear with my looks to live
extravagant throughout the world
If I was foolish could I place all intelligent people around me?
Would that make me smart, maybe then I
could cross another boundary
If I was just right for a ghetto black girl she would properly act white
Then she'll speak calmly fussing all night to
early light because I don't want to fight
If I'm crazy in love with a woman would she hold interest?
Or as soon as I'm tired of chasing her then
she'll want to be my mistress
If I'm tired of breaking the law and ready to settle down with family
Then the police would come running with
old warrants to chain up my sanity
If I don't want children will the woman of my dreams be fertile
Then discover after I change my mind her tubes are tied in circles
If I'm sick of being the man do I just convert to being a woman?
Then sorry good for nothing men escaping responsibility
can lie on their back and get money
If I'm born in a situation can I change it just because?
Some things you can others it can be excused
as that's just the way it was

The Red Word in the Blue Mind

Words Words Words
Well words can never turn Red until the end of your time reading
Similar to breathing out a cool frosty
breathe in the new dead of winter
But before then never knew which way the wind blew
When seeing is believing like crystal clear water turned into red wine
Blown minds of those who hear a written prose,
and captured posing in motions,
From revelations of my time here.
And as deep filled blue oceans so is the mind
that engulf, stop it that is enough
A word that is forged in the fires of adversity
must now pour like the days of Noah
Drowning out what was ignored and unheard
Causing people herding to the shore, so all would know for sure
So let me have a word with you till the end of your time reading

The Rose That Grew Through Concrete

Part III
The last rose that grows where nobody knows
Well I suppose if it's exposed tis best to look out my windows
I see out my soul I'm underneath feet hold me
down, light shines in the cracks of concrete
When I reach my peak, I will speak, and what was
frail and weak will appear strong and unique
It will be similar to bouquets that meet from the
same hill filled with dandy lions and daffodils.
And white lilies and this red rose with no sluggish will
It was hard to kill, cut off, put in the hole so
deep, to see it leap out was holy
Started off so lowly, but had to grow no
one watched as it came up slowly
Now behold me, who has slept under a project
bed were the roaches and rats run
No other place allowed me to come, blessed to
have a creepy place to sleep in the slums
Never forget where you come from, from
young bum to the riches of the wise
Still I rise towards sunny skies till my demise, in every cell saving lives
We must realize dreams come from on high,
to where my hard plastic pillows lie
We must reply, do or die, fail or succeed either way we must try
So why in the hell are so many held back, Only God can testify
Because between you and I we all got stories
to tell from hardships similar to jail

We must prevail till all is well as a fresh green
steam and bright red rose petal
That wouldn't settle till it grew through concrete,
razor sharp barbwire and rusty heavy metal

Dedicated to 3000 victims of Sept. 11

Twin Tower's fallen down

It seemed I went to sleep in one world and awoke in another
The day went like any other; I got up to go to the trade center as usual
I have this great job at the twin towers; I enter the subway as always
Read the papers on the way hoping the
new secretary say good day 2 me
Grab my briefcase and walk inside work, its early ready for coffee
In the office just another day as time tick,
some people in another place,
are being taken hostage or being killed but
what has that got 2 do with me
But when disasters strikes and collide with the innocent in the middle
It makes for a raging aftermath an ending horrific and tragic
Back to me spinning around in my leather
swivel chair and then the beginning
A loud deafen noise that struck a pose of we all going to die
Flashing lights, flicker and the burning jet
fumes get thick out my wildest dreams
Hearing screams and hollering, co-workers
running and falling all crazy
A nightmarish scene you wouldn't believe
unless you seen it for yourself
The floor collapse from underneath and the sprinklers spray overhead
It makes a sizzling sound as the melting frame
and floor comes crumbling down
Today will have its way, I will not awake, and it's no happy ending
So I take a picture of my family out pray as I cough and gag
No this can't be happening, what just
happened, smoke out the window

People throw themselves out the top to keep from burning alive
What will quench this fire that's consuming
fire extinguisher, metal and all?
Is this hell opening itself up for me to swallow me whole?
Then I look again and see an old friend that's passed long ago
He was a righteous man who I knew went to heaven, and said it's ok.

Unspoken Wordz

I don't have to shout I love you for you to know
It should blurt out of turn, through blatantly action it'll show
If I was ferociously angry then my cruel silence would be felt
You shouldn't have to guess if I'm mad atcha quiet is kept
Do you really feel my vibes and passion I hide inside
Read between the lines, these symbols and signs have cried
Expression must abide, through subtle ways they leak and appear
Through body language blasphemy and abomination becomes clear
What am I still doing here? Is the question you need 2 ask yourself
What he or she did with their body and say they love you,
Anyone else would have left
But you intensely listen to their wordz
Manipulation, deeply sinking into screaming sorry is all you heard
We all have different agendas, so miss me with the speech
I teach judge by action, wordz are so far out of reach
I don't have to tell you I'm alone you should
know in this twilight zone
I'm in, like love ones turn their back and gone in the midnight
Home is where they're on the way to, and I've grown to dislike
What I'm shown, so I take heed and proceed with caution on sight
And believe half of what I see and none of what I hear
So be careful friends, family, and countrymen,
when they say lend me your ear

Chapter V

After you've done all you can do

Jewel 141: A small decision can be trivial and may not seem like it has a lasting effect, however these choices that can easily to either way; later down the road can be so detrimental. It could change our lives forever.

Dedication to Pastor Gregory Black
And Anthony P. Grice

Amen

The prodigal son on the run in a foreign Land
It's in every man to get his belongings and leave home
The fight is on the hunger to achieve much better
A great father will let his son go out on his own
O.K you're grown here is what's yours, Take care now
Are you listening are you out there, is anybody else lost
It comes a time when every man must find his way
Thank God sees it and guides it with his all seeing eye
4 God leads us across wicked lands safe and sound
The son was lost, but now has found his way back
In the black of night on a black rock crawls a black ant
And God sees that too! And reveals our secrets in our heart
So what am I in this hellish world standing all alone?
So much Lord we don't miss until it's gone AMEN 2 that

Bowels of Hell

This condition is a massive understatement, of misery and insanity that plagues the feelings of a political prisoner; being held in solitary confinement. He can't help his screams to the top of his lungs trying to drown out the sounds of voices from which he can never succumb. Is this a nightmare dream? The theme is bone crunching killings, bone chilling emotions come running to quench his pain he's addicted to. Telling him to self- inflict injury it'll be delicious. Trying to convince his self, one pain can cancel out another. An Ocean of tears to drown in is worthy punishment for one. Ready to perish in grief, having heard of such suffering makes the ears of the listener tingle and pop, leaving a soul to shake and quiver in electric shock, Warm agony begin sprinkling across his mind, till the top burst, flames of fire rain down with brimstone in this dark cavity of a curse. The solitude and despair falls thick around. The prisoner fiendish desires speaks of escaping, plotting with his self in a muffled breathe, and husky voice. Deeply knowing it's no escape, he's got no choice but to simply exist, and be. The only alternative is to gouge out both eyes so he can no longer see. This madness and chaos that's left him drenched and burnt simultaneously. Longing to be in the hell that Dante mentioned compared to this, that's paradise. But here is blood where bodies burst because it can no longer stand the pressure, similar to spontaneous combustion, pain explode inside as a migraine in the mind that fester. Hollers, screams and echoes of noises that sound like a wild animal that feeds and eats and rips meats that need no more bleed, then the time comes of great silence, piercing and eerie, and lonely. Only his breathe left to accompany him. Then as an avalanche comes flooding, bring the noise of a freight train. Shrieks, and screams from the killings and then the political prisoner in solitary confinement can't help, but scream to the top of his lungs to drown out the voices and the sounds of the perpetual killings lasting throughout eternity.

Cradle 2 the Grave

When every soul was born out the primeval ocean
On a journey that has been truly amazing, an adventure
This would change the face of the physical life plane here
As life came clear from there to travel in a sperm cell
With millions and millions of brothers
and sisters survival of the fittest
All squiggly and squirmy with a tail, head straight for the egg
This through inside of protoplast has a ways before it get legs
Inside the egg all alone, no one else made it, it grows as an embryo
So time moves slow out here, but inside her millions of years
Evolution at its best, and in 12 weeks or less it's a fetus
We all are just old souls, hid behind 9 months inside
Then we finally arrive and say we're only a day old
Put us in a cradle and nourish us with milk from the nipple
Ohh we grow so fast we are from past life time's ago
Then the baby learns to walk, talk, and have a dream
But the truth is as the baby grows it dies a little every day
Time whizz by, all kinds of pictures from graduation to marriage
Till now you've witness another little one in a carriage by you
You've made it through some good times and bad times too!
Now gray hair is on your head and from the fight to the egg
One must learn to embrace him or herself
cause you are all you have left
In death to the grave

Dedicated to a Friend of Mine

You know who you are, you know what you did through my bid
When I was locked down as a rabid animal in the lost and found
Your concern was enough for me to make it through times tough
Love was sent in the mail just telling me of all is well
I could never repay or thank you fully, every day you was there
My friend to the end ha! You say, that's not even the half
Even after we're gone our friendship will go on through family
They'll tell stories of us around a dinner table just to pass the time
Dedicated to a friend of mine you know good n well who you is
You've been around for awhile always kiss and smile for me
What you doing now I wonder, we made it
through hail, rain, and thunder
You never gave up on me I dedicate this work to Joyce Thomas
Amazing as you are shiny star in this dark, dreary, gloomy night
It's no words I can put together, or I've heard to say 4ever
You are my friend to the end of time home girl, believe that
As I sat and wrote this I heard somebody quote this
It was going to be some sweet times going down, friend of mine
Nobody can ever take your place, ohh how I love your face
You always did what you could true blue till I made it through
And let me say this loud and clear you're the reason why I'm still here
You selected me, and protected me like earth angels suppose to do.

Evolution

Its name is evolution, a driven calculated machine
The things that you dream of, it actually
does and goes through with it
Living in a world beyond our world, 50 moves ahead without limit
Unflinching moving forward with precision and extreme passion
It knows no substitute for greatness, it never fails 2 deliver
There's nothing that stand in its way its execution is flawless
So lawless as it stares down the most authoritated and it's intimidated
Bow your head in the presence of evolution, it looked at me
To make it happen is the tool it use to defuse the situation
With its deadly concentration on everything seen at 1st glance
It's no second chance to escape from an unescapable reality
So it mastered the art of destiny and embraced as its 1st love
Making something priceless out of nothing, job well done
Acting in moments of desperation, with an imaginary gun to its head
Watch out, its name is evolution and nothing can change its effect

Grown Woman

You said you was no longer a naïve little girl, you ready 4 the world
Time has changed since you wore bright
beads and Shirley Temple curls
Wearing pink pearls and your mamas slippers
walking around acting grown
Now baby you on your own, when things go
wrong; can't keep running home
When you're all alone and this so called poor
excuse of a man has gone cheating.
Remain strong, don't accept the beatings, you
can do bad by yourself, I keep repeating
Fall to your knees and ask God to guide your
every step in this crocked way
Then ask for help to stay and he leaves, please God sincerely we pray
Don't worry about the bills fill the bag up with all his shoes and cloths
Even though you're angry don't burn or cut'em,
just leave them out doors exposed
The man or your dreams is on the other end
watching knowing one day you'll get fed up
Respecting that it's not his place to tell you to
get rid of him just keep your head up
But when he's gone then he can come in like the fresh summer wind
And say now let us begin, through thick
and thin baby, I'll be your friend
He's been across the street watching, waiting
for his opportunity the whole time
From this opportunity came this moment that
seemed tragic, but was really divine
Take a chance to advance this moment that
seemed tragic, but was really divine

Take a chance to advance a grown woman
must act under certain circumstance
If you love him, but he don't show love to
you, look elsewhere for romance
As men glance at a woman you can tell she's
independent and holds her own
Don't need any help from any man, only
in God cause she's fully grown
It was a grown woman that shown me the way to being a grown man
To take care of home, family first, and make sure we do all we can?
To please each other in every way known to mind, body and soul
And if this isn't happing in your life now,
then someone is out of control

I Am

I am God
But surely not the most high
I am odd
But nobody tells me why
I am truth
But some will say I'm a lie
I am proof
But dumb folks still look in the sky
I am a scene
But spoke of as a dream
I am a theme
But don't' be moved by my extreme
I am thought
But don't' think about me in form
I am caught
But like fleeting winds I'm gone
I am crazy
But that's what the foolish say
I am amazing
But people didn't see me that way

Dedicated to Elvis A. Presley

I Forgot 2 Remember 2 Forget

I thought about her and dialed her phone number
As I almost forgot to remember to forget about her
A hazy blur, it seemed everything was as it was before
Then memories pour in we threw in the towel, we're no more
Ride to the store and go to the cooler and get flowers she like
Almost to her house, put on the signal light then remember
Before I enter her drive way, that it was
weeks ago that I had to end her
Chunk the flowers out and continue about feeling stung
My conversation has not quit rolling her name off my tongue
I catch myself before I call on her as she's not in the picture
Embarrassed then smile when the thought finally hitcha
As I turn over in the bed to wrap my arms around her waist
My hand hit the wall and I awake to a pillow with no pillow case
I sit up in the bed about to hear who's in the kitchen
Then remember she's not in the refrigerator, no more I listen
A car pull up in the front is she home from work
I snatch back the curtains at the window it's not her
She's long gone, and I forgot to remember to carry on.
End of the story poor me, she's still in my system so strong
Must I put a sign up as reminder to not to forget
So I'll remember it's over today, I forgot as I sent her a text

Jewel. 113. Perfection should not always be a distant goal, but at some point a present day new standard to be held to; and those that within a set time do not measure up should be held accountable.

The life that we are blessed with and given the responsibility to push humanity to the next level can't be taken lightly. Everyday we should be thinking about what is it I can do today to contribute to the cause of fallen humanity. It is only the dream of the weak and poor minded to only get rich, but the real wealth is built up in the compilation of time and what we as individuals did in our life time to bring us to the next level. In fact It is the purpose of each and everyone of us to withstand the test of time and when the opposition gets in our way push further for the purpose that we were divinely created. As Jesus purpose was to bring the stage of humanity to a spiritual level of positivity and of good will, so in each and every one of use have the same identity to fulfill. My mission statement on this earth is to bring a positive change in the darkness with the resonating light that each and every one of us already have in us. As most know my story already, my struggles and my strength and weakness, through all the cold sweats and night terrors continue remember always persist on. Never forget who you are and never forget your purpose, and if you see someone or something try your damn best to get it.

Laughing in the Face of Death

Entry # 5

Ha! Ha! It's funny that man must write his life off.

Like an unpaid bill what's the deal with the pay off.

Did he conquer dreams by any means did he achieve.

How many grieve in the end cause we had to leave.

Man is not the body or the soul, but a part of Allah.

And Allah is a spirit and death can never face Allah.

Ha! Ha! So he bust out laugh and grab the attention of a friend.

And tell him to listen to this, death tries to bring an end.

Then he laughs too as they carry on like nothing matter.

Even though it seems bad Ha! Ha! Nothing else really matters.

Because though I walk through the valley of shadows of death.

I shall fear no evil, Satan coming from my right and left.

From the front and back trying to cause me to deviate.

But it's too late for me; it's nothing to cause me to deviate.

Now as for the man that was told the lo and behold.

I'll give you power to tread upon serpents and scorpions.

And nothing by any means shall hurt you (son of God)

Says the Lord

Dedicated to Stacy Lynn. Thomas

My Bed in Hell

I was wrapped up in the depths of misery; as far as I could see
A blanket of lies and betrayal covered me; that was short 2 my knee
Smelled like stale pee, and a hard bottom
that left my back in soar pains
When will I rise again off this mattress of
madness for the criminally insane?
Yet I sustain when I see this beautiful Angelic
face in this brimstone place
She reaches out and touch me like God's
grace and I'm about to be embraced
My oversized pillow case loses the miniature
pillow that's plastic and hard
Forcing oneself to lay in such drastic measures
to get sleep is outside God
Sleep on little kiddy sleepers that have made your hard bed in hell
But an Angel came to see me there, and calmed the cries and wail

Dedicated to Debbie Trump

My Charming Tormentor II

I hate that we couldn't have met under different circumstances
Wishing we could have at least been good friends though
Maybe in another life, but no need 2 beat myself up?
God has a funny twisted sense of humor, ha! ha!
Yeah!! I always get what I don't want without asking
And the things I ask for sincerely, I'll never smell it.
Hell she don't even trust me, then she bends over backwards 4 me
I'm sure with her mood swings some can't stand her
While I beckon to her every whim
Drinking her bath water doesn't says nearly enough
Worshipping the ground she walks on whoa
whoa whoa that's way too much
4 a real woman wants a real man, to be cool and nonchalant.
Not crazy, acting silly and foolishly deranged over love.
But be able to provide 4 her in every way and give her
unimaginable pleasures 4 a life time.
I'll go suffer now the thought that I have 2 leave prison
and my enchanted love will go her way to forget me.
I feel so much better now that I've been beat in open shame
I've came along ways just 2 see her in hell.
And she only torment me the more with the silent treatment
then she'll talk and laugh and she sees who I am.
That's O.K I thank God to have met such a woman.
The End

Dedicated to Emmett Till

O.J go Free

I know you did it, I can see it in your belligerent eyez
You might as well Emmett it, because in the end everybody dies
Nicole was quite a beauty in disguise she could have fooled me
She humiliated you, now she's dead her boyfriend too! O.J go Free
If it doesn't fit you must acquit no double
Jeopardy miss me with the bull#$?t lies
The authorities tampered with evidence to convict you for taking lives
Bloody rags, gloves the wrong size yeah that was a big mistake
Not realizing that the crime scene to make was another life to take
Police was hard to shake when you lead them on a wild goose chase
Race against time as you cleared your mind, and got to save face
Thought it over and while everything on pace according to plan
Cops thought they had their man but guilt
don't show because you ran
Even if you told lies being a liar don't make you the killer
If judges are the death dealer, then Johnnie Cochran is a death healer
His plea of not guilty I imagine shocked the entire world
Why? Because he got away with killing one poor innocent white girl
What about the slaughter of us even after slavery killing our kind
And the white world turned a blind eye the atrocities blew our mind
Hanging us, then say later yeah I did it that gets me
Looking at a white woman can get you killed, yet O.J go Free.

MARVIN THOMAS

Precious Hard Times

As he pray to God he don't lose his minimum wage job tonight
Times are tight and they're firing and laying off on the job site
The lights are off so he borrowed hot water from the neighbors
To take a bath and rest fresh from his tiresome labors
And there's no food to eat it hasn't been for many days
So he sits in the dark and pick through left over trays
Mama sent him some good home ole-fashion cooking last weekend
What was left over is spoiled and got the whole house reeking
Candles lite by an open window with a battery operated fan
To lay with his girl in front of on the sheetless bed 2 devise a plan
Soon eviction notice come in, tears are cried from his woman
Before the phone cut off, from bill collectors he was running
Repo man came for the car with no gas in the tank
How do he thank he's going to move his things, He can't
How do he plan to get back and forth to where he work
No way to mama's house, now his pocket's empty and belly hurt
Outside the grass is grown up like nobody live there
It's a good place to lay and hide after ducking cab fare
But he can't afford to get to work unless he had a bike
Or sleep in the storage room at the job late at night
Tell his woman stay with her people till it get better
His poor job gives him walking papers in bad weather
After being fired he leaves walking in rain to no home, it's gone
To nowhere, alone then he says precious hard times I've known.

Rooted and Grounded

I see myself carved in you.
Are you Arabian?
Wood from the Niles of Blue.
Can't be Canadian.
Your Beauty is crystal clear.
With no Mist
Our life spans on this time table.
That turns and twist.
God's knife cuts me into you
A Roman sculpture.
So I lie on this canvas sinking.
As ink erupture
On a perfect oil painted picture
Like Mona Lisa
Your flawless face is a work of art
Japanese geisha
Rooted and grounded through
Grooves in our body.
Language that tastes exquisite.
Silver Bacardi
Grown in each other.
As blue engrave plants of Cuba
Tatto of a perfect moment
Lay deeply within you

Sistah Soulja

Do you got plans to hold me down, and get a dude from out of town
In case you want your tummy touched every then and now
Tell'em shush don't make a sound when I call
Will you be there if I need anything at all?
Be sure he wears a fitted when you let him hit it
Don't let your friends tell me you be first to admit it
Send me some flicks and a few dollars for some new kicks
And when I touch down I want listen to
those lies from those cheap tricks
Never put him in a ride or crib that I paid for
Get a room keep it zoom what you stayed for
Tell him straight up about you and me and what's it gonna be
When I come home every know that he gotta leave
Don't bring him around my kid when I'm on my bid
You know in V-I he gonna tell me everything you did
If it's getting too much for you be a woman and let me know
Don't be a hoe hanging up the phone trying to let me go
If you ride for two or three that's all I can ask
I'll remember everything you did for me when you run out of gas
No family members no one I deal with, you know the rules
Call me fool while you screw the world as
long as they don't touch my girl
Put letters and pic's in your pocketbook so
when he scramble for loose change,
For cigarettes even though he's mad it
makes it hard for him to explain
He can fall in love if he want to just do what I told ya
And I'll take care of everything when I get home to my sistah soulja

Thatz Crazy

We often hear something that don't sounds like what we're use to
Then we'll say thatz crazy, but my question is according to who
Yeah! Thatz crazy what those two burglars up and did
Broke into a home and found pornography of some kids
The burglars jumped up and called the police, turned the owner in
Thatz crazy people break into his house and turn him in
Even if they fall and hurt their self on your property
Under certain circumstances they can sue, so proceed carefully
Don't shoot if they break in and they turn around and run
Are they all the way in the house clear, do they have a gun
If not then you'll go to prison for involuntary manslaughter
And just like a flounder fish fresh out of water
Out of nowhere you're locked up and didn't even do nothing
Like a homie said one time you might as well do something

Thatz Crazy

Long Kiss Good-bye

I'm not going to start this epic poem out by recording vicious lies
She wasn't a beauty queen, at times though easy on the naked eyez
I recognized this inner beauty that told the story of all great men
To look deep within to find the precious life to help one ascend
She was a blonde headed white woman
that had a tarnish tooth in front
She was what I had, notice seldom you ever get who you want
A thick bone, pale tone with glasses on, always stoned off weed
Continue to read, you'll find out it's not
what you want, it's what you need
Now let's proceed; she gave me lead on her place to temporary stay
So I moved my cloths in cause my bills in Creekside I couldn't pay
I can hear her say, save your money Mar and get yourself together
Times like these make apprehension of living
better seem like taking forever
I weathered the storm, now being at her house was the new norm
Even though I had cloths and furniture locked up in a storage barn
She had wild home girls, and my reckless
homeboys were wild as ever 2
Plus she had three kids and dog sitting her boss's dog in this zoo
How I make it through? Anywaayyyyy that's a complete nother story
I paid for it sorely, I lost a dog she was
babysitting she put me out (poor me)
Who could foresee me leaving out, left the back door half-cracked
While she was doing the weekend in the county jail, laid up on a rack
It seemed the deck was stacked against me in the game of life
My precious wife had left me; only thing stuck with me was strife
I lost my licenses for a DUI now I lost my girlfriend's dog
They repoed my Malibu too, and I lost my
second job chopping Parkers BBQ Hog's

Only McDonald's was there, and behind it
stood a new construction building
Where late night when I knocked off, I would
go to sleep with my track phone chilling
From day 2 day sometimes gray, sometimes blue, sometimes drunk
The horrific truth stunk as I wondered the streets it all sunk in
Searching for a missing dog that deep down I knew wasn't there
I'm hoping through all the nightmare nights as early dew she'll care
Every freaking where I peeped and came up
short, so now slowly I'm taught
The lessons of life is take care of the precious things already caught
And things roaming around on the dark green grass on the other side
Let it ride, be content with what you have, at your place abide
From house to house my homeboyz on pity would often take me in
Or some overweight chick on section 8 attempt
to make me have sex to sleep in the den
This is only a little hell I've been through, true story no sike
Like riding on a bike in the rain, from job to job late night
Or in no lights on, where scarily home cooked food reaches my belly
On McDonalds Big Mac's or quick fix sandwiches from the deli
Feet don't fail me now, as often I take the long walk across town
To the storage barn to exchange my clothes or see who's around
One day my girl sees me and afterwards lets me sleep over
I've been robbing with my comrades to pay
for the dog is what I told her
And after I showed her all the things that I had seen and done
I'm having a good run, but dayz later I'll disappear for a stolen gun
So she embraced me slowly and let me weasel my way back in
I'm acting like now I'm in love more than I ever been
Smoking weed and drinking beer induced into the smoky night
As I delicately laid her on her junky bed ohh ever so lightly

Like it was going to be the very last time I would touch her body
Caressing her softly in sporadic movements to say I'm sorry
Kissing her, missing her like never before to re-enter her nest
Ohh yes, this time is more or less what we could have been at best
Yes, like for the first time, this is nothing like the times before
When in the beginning had her and didn't
want her and now want her even more
Cause this maybe a one night stand, just to explore possibilities
If it's really me she's wants or her ex-boyfriend in the penitentiary
Either or tomorrow she'll drop me off in her black Cherokee
To Mickey D's she'll go to work till evening for me it's to Sheetz
I open the door and gaze at her like I will see her no more
In front of the store, she laughed and said Mar, What's the look 4
What's the matter with me for some strange reason I want a kiss
I had to sale this last gun and then get across town before I miss-
My homeboy Brien that's going to give me a car radio for her truck
So I'm stuck in her glance, I pucker up my round thick lips
And slowly kiss her passionately as a man on a one way no return trip
Pushing my tongue out tasting the madness
to come from the last time
Lips locked intertwined slipped tongue into hers from mine
It seemed divine for a few seconds, so intense so fairy tale real
To feel her actually love me for the first time,
and have to go make this deal
No sooner her tires squeal off, I begin to try to sale this piece of steel
And as fate would tell the story it seems I approached an off duty cop
I stopped him, he didn't stop me and long story short I got popped
Hauled me off to jail and tried to get ole girl to post my bail
But by it being a million dollars, I don't
think so (it's time to wish me well)

So after a few weeks she told me on collect
calls you know where I'll be
It's not like I'm going to be out whoring in these Greenville streets
Get yourself together, do your time because here come the feds
Get out and then come find me, this is what she said
So after a few hung up phones, no answered letters, now this
All I had to hang on to was that moment
of Good-by in the Long Kiss

Wacko Jacko goes Free

Did you enjoy the little boy, who can ask if he did?
No one can say I know you did it, had sex with a kid
And to be frank, I felt like he knew more than came out
Your argument was everyone was lying on
you, Willis what you talking about
I've seen him in bedroom shoes show up for court late
Does star power do that, attempting to make the judge wait
Deciding his fate was a joke to him as the world set and watched
Innocent little boys layed in his bed with nothing on but socks
It was said that the experience at the mansion was sweet
The come up was for the little boy family who got put on their feet
Some say it was an out of court settlement for undisclosed cash
The price for the little boy . . . holding secrets was a discreet pass
O.K you got off and the judge heard the jury plea of not guilty
Little boyz was his life, that almost destroyed him Jacko go free
All on T.V with the extended nose and a veil over his face
It seemed like he would have a reputation for boyz after the case
Even if he didn't do it, people will say he did on T.V
That's a bad bone to have on anybody, Wacko Jacko goes free

Long Live the Possum

We are only young for a moment, then like
wine drunk out of a goblet, we're gone.
Gobbled up time moves on, reminiscent thoughts become our home
No more flesh and bone to rely on, just memories
Remember these poems as deep as Middle Eastern Seas.
Legacies past down from men on knees sent straight through my eye.
Telling me one day youngster when the time is right, I too will rise.
While demise is promised to me, I must continue on to pass the ring
So we might one day all be connected, beyond the DNA strand.
That's the one thing expected as we all search
for a freedom that's in our dream.
Or what foolish old men speak of, in what they seen but couldn't hold
So we unfold tomorrow chasing the hope that we was told.
Be bold in our living, leaving behind wings
spread on gold rays of light.
I wish I could have done more, Long Live the Possum

Chapter VI

The Master who knew nothing at the Start.

Jewel 144: When a man is locked up it could be next to impossible to get a $100 sent in. Love is not a factor when financial stability is absent from the outside. The reality is a rinky dink job out in society makes for empty promises sent in and a grade 1 job the answer to your prayers.

Anguish of a lonely Man

Somebody wake me I'm dreaming, cause
I'm seeing angels and demons
And I'm a victim screaming afraid to look,
because of these sick twisted beings.
Why am I here why must a man that try so hard to do well
Fail in his endeavors and find himself way in heaven and hell.
Jail may have even been sweeter if I hadn't tasted life outside.
Many tried to cope and adjust, and lied to themselves to abide.
Guide me God to find a better way since I've found loved ones
A family to come home to and from with the light of the sun
Done got myself in a little struggle, but by no fault of my own
It seems some men are prone to victimization till their gone
Alone in this suffering atmosphere what we have here hurts
Words that flirt with suicidal thoughts, what's it all worth
At times it seems I've made it, and victory becomes plain and sure
Pure madness sometimes excites internal riots making death allure
I must endure all the pain and pressure for my girls I love
In the above dark clouds where there is no sunshine just because
God of light and darkness keep us blinded with bright truth and lies
The skies may appear dreary and pitched why must I close my eyes
Cries from a man of strength written on these pages you read
My pen bleeds like my old battle scars making your eyes heed
To the need of my understanding, and don't label me bad
I was snatched from the best life I ever had, now I'm mad
Only to grab a cigarette, but I don't smoke choke then cough
I'm lost without the guidance of God; Jesus carried the cross
For me and you off to Calvary he went to perish for us.
So now who can I trust, if this life of sin is blind?
Attacking the mind of men trying to do well most of the time.

BROKEN WINGZ

They say mistakes are to teach you how to
reach a plateau of being wise.
The pinnacle of wisdom even was started from
the bottom and it 2 had to rise.
Hard lessons we all learned from fire embraced
into our bosom 2 get burned.
No need 2 holler now but this should make
you have cause for concern.
No one can get another in trouble peer pressure
is to test you, make up your mind.
Don't be blind nor listen to friends trying to coerce you into crime.
Time to cross the line now every man must
now or never make a stand.
Either rob and steal all you can or deviate from
the plan and get a helping hand.
From the family and can be enjoying the
freedoms that come with sacrifice.
Hard heads makes for a hard bed in prison,
but you can't lay down in life.
Many depend on a girlfriend who says she'll be there no matter what.
Till a pair of cuffs him, then she'll tell you she hate your guts.
Now she's gone with the wind as a feather, 2 love is 2 let go
If you know what you now know from
spectacular mistakes you would grow.
Stay strong, after all failures and pitfalls you can still truly rise.
And see the world from the heights of heaven with eagle eyez.
Instead of lie down we must excel at alarming
rates, and not just get by.
No matter how many scars and hurt, spread
those broken wingz and fly.
The struggle and challenge may be extreme flawless damage.
Rise above it all and elevate with a wing bruise and bandage.

Dedicated to
Gloria Jean Thomas

Dear Mom

Mom is the name of God on the lips every child
Ohh look how you made me smile as I thought about you for awhile
I seen you as a night owl processing chickens on 3rd shift
If I had one wish it's to take away painful
memories and give you God's gift
When I was little and got lost at Kings Dominions,
I never thought I'll see your face again
When you found where I been, you gave me
the most precious slap I ever had
I knew you was glad to see me, even though I made you mad
You know dad haven't always been there for me
But it don't matter cause I know my mother love me
Despite when I cut up acting bad as hell,
at Christmas you never failed
Always first day of school I was dressed very well
Even though I broke the rules since you bless me with good looks
I acted cool, I was a whole lot smarter than
I looked, yet played the fool
Like one night behind the wheel, stole my mom Bonneville.
Don't care about cops if she catches me she's goona kill me?
Neil was gone from home, no one else to look at
but in the review mirror at the real me
Memories of when I bought you a China vase on Mother's day
Memories of how I took to Edna Andrews your income tax pay
Memories of a liar cheat and a roach is what you say
All cause I will not obey
These are memories of my mom in the month of May.

Dedicated to Adam and Eve

Foolish Passions

Your passion was so erotic and mystic
From the moment you poked it out, and I kissed it
I felt tabooed and jaded, and my thoughts were elated
So I just stepped backed and stared at it and gazed
Thoughts running wild what it could do 2 me
Would it capture me enrapture me, set my appetite a blaze
Then I touched it with my fingers ever so lightly
Then it spoke satisfy your curiosity, don't try 2 fight me
The fragrance smelling like a fresh fruit orchard
2 not be able to press my nose against it is psychological torture
Exotic emotions stimuli my mental high
A perfect picture begins 2 soothe the apple of my eye
She said take a nibble just a little then stop
Sweet flavors ready 2 burst into the cream of the crop
Juices on top, I can't take it, I resist no longer
The urge of my infatuation grows much stronger
Mouthwatering I can already taste, I see a smile on her face
Then I dig in and I'm feeling next 2 God
As I exquisitely bite a portion from this pod
Then as my eyes open we both look at each other
and think what have we just done?

Guilty Pleasures

He thought her boyfriend was going to shoot
him in the face when they drove up.
To the laundry mat she told him, don't worry just put my cloths up?
As he pulled up beside them, he had been waiting around the corner
This devious little woman, grabbed a cloths
basket, and changed her persona
Started cursing him out, acting mad as they were caught red handed
She made him feel like he was acting foolish and
jealous, stupidity she couldn't stand it
No need to panic as he walked back to the
car, head hung down shame face
Since him and his girl were best friends with them,
and later would visit each other place
However he and his friend's girlfriend had just left a sleazy hotel
Whew that was a close call; all went well now the story to tell
They always flirted with each other; ole girl blew kisses on the low
When her old man back was turned, and
of course his girl didn't know
So the chase begin and for years on her shoulder he cried tears
He told her of his inactive sexual relation
with his girl, and he had fears
So he went into therapy telling of all of the
sexual problems with his girl
Not knowing that at the end of his recovery
was seeing down a double barrel
He begged help me the only other option
was go out and catch a disease
So she let him squeeze on her and kiss her till they both were pleased
Till she finally broke years later and allowed
him the full experience, she cried

The best friend of his girl opened up the
final door to let him come inside
Now they had to act weird as nothing happened
when they all were together again
Both feeling guilty pleasures as they continued
further and further to pretend.

I Won

As I stumble through this dry and barren desert
Feeling exhausted and depleted of all liquids
So dehydrated that I would gladly drink my own warm urine,
If there was any to hurry and pour out
The heat thumps and beat upon my head
As a thousand drums, to punish the sins of the whole world
I'm so so tired, but I stagger on.
My legs continue to intensely cramp but move forward, why I ask?
Seeing in them the will to live is strong
One would think if they were to see me afar
This limp body on top was a corpse
Carried by a pair of robotic legs and feet
My mind is delirious and dumbfounded
And pain that stings my inner strength has become my friend
I'm thankful that the buzzards hover over to give
Me shade under their beautiful wings of dark shadows
The illusion of rain drops automatic causes my tongue to wag out
I hear my heartbeat, and my breathe
I lock-up and fall to the earth, like a sack of potatoes
With the last ounce of strength I widen my
eyelids to look forward ahead
I see a green valley with a pond by it, and the hot
scorching sand feels good it doesn't hurt anymore
                              I whisper I won.

KKK

Why do you hate us so much, is it that you think I'm not clean
Well it's no such thing as an unclean people cause of color
Your dreams are to smother, hang and choke out the dark man
Why do your grudge runs so deep when nobody done nothing to you
Your people were the ones that enslaved mine, we should have the hate
Instead they rather propagate this faith of white is right
Superior plan of God and everybody else is under your foot stool
One rule under the Klu Klux Klan, and where would we all be
Had my ancestors not come and built up this land that's so great
You make old wounds dry hard when the Klan continues to hate
What really make you hate our guts, kill'em all is how the KKK feel
Call us Niggers, well maybe that's the harshest word ever heard
Your inbreed hate has no bounds and no dominions
My question is why you wear those white sheets over your face
Wouldn't you want everybody to discover your identity you represent
Is that what you was taught to crucify him, well that makes him great
Like Jesus was crucified by the stake or some say tree
Hang to death this is the freedom that we all shall get
Don't think your violent crimes will go unjudged, no they want
Kill him my forefathers hear Klan screams come cross the field
Your children are bread that hate, taught not to feel anything
Maybe that's why sometimes your children grow up killing you

Ded 2
The Prophet Noble Drew Ali

Love, Truth, Peace, Freedom and Justice

Honesty is the most precious virtue a man can ever have
So grab the truth as it's passed down generously to you from me
No water down, but blood raw, it's ever clear what I've seen
Screams of individuals having nightmares
wake up ask what's going on
I'm shown the terror of time chasing these fragile young black males
Crack sales and possession of pistols don't
warrant the extermination of us
Plus you got aids and these drugs and guns putting in over time
I'll shine a light into the night, and it's no telling what you might see
We must show more love, now that's a big word heard some don't like
Right is right, wrong is wrong true love is given for none in return
It's a cause for deep concerns, to not love family in such a way
Thrown away keys locked up makes freedom seem as a distant dream
Let freedom ring is what king said, for it
he was sent back to the essence
I've become obsessed with finding justice or
is it just us that commit crimes
Time will tell as truth prevail and unveil the two scales of paradox
Lock down in a cell block till they release
you; look at you scream chow
No way no how, I'm coming here again, less
I'm choked out, wake up here
A tear fall from these eyez as memories collide with those in the world
The girl I want is a convict; the one that wants me is way too old
Will my soul ever find peace, maybe not till I carry a piece?
And cease to function in the chaos and confusion of this plane

Can't wait to sang, I want to go outside, and go outside in the sun
The one prophet Noble Drew Ali has given me purpose and reason
So now I'm leaving, but far from being done, look 4 me
I came in love and I leave in peace

Dedicated to Debbie Trump

My Charming Tormentor

It was strange how we met, my beloved I'll never forget
We are from 2 different eras, ages, and obscure generations.
Yet we made it to meet each other on this journey
I know I wasn't supposed to but by time and chance
It's been a nightmare of a living hell 2 not be able to,
Touch her, or look at her the way I want to do
She probably haven't had a lot of experience
with a man such as myself but ohh well
All I can do to keep from going insane from her whippings
That is write my feelings to a cold world, then die in peace
I loathe the fact that I can't feel intensely inside her
As she extremely should be felt every part every inch of her
She's the most peculiar and cutest person I've ever seen
And I'm not talking about looks so she shouldn't flatter herself
I'm talking about her personality and how she carries herself
The way she wears all black most time is in harmony with her skin
My pains I bare having to stare down when I really want 2
I want to look into her big bright crystal eyez
Even though she's probably old enough to be my mother
I simply don't care; it's her mind that appeals to me
The body is just a reflection of who she resemble
And I'm not afraid to look anymore even though it hurtz
2 be continued . . .

My Love for you

My love for you is pure and madly intense at times
As chimes are blown by the wind so have you blown my mind
Intertwine my thoughts of you of all kinds
My love for you is not blind but clear as noon day sunshine
With the fine tune vision of our life almost ready for the world to see.
It's you and me baby; I love you like you love me.
I want you so bad I can taste you in my mouth
My soul aches and cramps for you when you're away
When my love is all about.

On the Eve of our Blind Date

I know you can't wait 2 meet me
Just like I can't wait 2 meet you
But we don't have the time or luxury
So we're just going to have to make do
Beyond this veil, it's not hard 2 tell that it's see through
But you know goodness well
Now it's our world and our time
Look with me through this blind fold
Never mind me
But I'm willing 2 bet my soul
Where ever you are you'll find me
Watching over you
But let me introduce myself 1st
I'm the one, Jehovah's sun, I'm a Super Nova
I'm a star ready to burst
In the woman that holds the mysteries
of the whole universe
From better through worst
To the blessed and the cursed baby
I rather eat and die with you
Then live life alone daily

Prisoner and the Butterfly

A crystal clear perfect sky, through it a fresh scent pass-by
Spring evergreen forests bud out, crisp leaves in the scenery
Echoes of the distant winter no longer hover, but discover love
Out in this open field is a stone wall building surrounded by iron
A metal barb wire fence, and it's dull and gloomy on sight
Inside men wear brown khakis or gray jogging suits.
It's in the cool of the day and people walk outside in this.
Walking the track, some post up reading books on benches.
But it was one who set under a little tree and observed.
In his own world nothing else mattered as people scattered.
It was silence and the prisoners moved in slow motion
The one prisoner under the little tree intensely looked on.
Then as a moment in a twinkle of the eye there it was.
In elaborate details and vivid colorful features it flew.
As the wind rustled and blew, it fluttered in with the wind.
This beautiful butterfly one like he had never seen before.
Has something like this ever been as it drew closer.
These high definition rainbow colors of red, orange, and yellow.
The butterfly seem to glitter and sparkle off the sunlight.
It set on a branch in the proximity of eye view.
Seemingly to be staring at each other in curiosity.
Both thinking as in the still not to move, and what are you?
The prisoner pointed his finger out wondering would he land on it.
But the Butterfly could take no chance and flew away.

Rise 2 the Call

If needed I'm the man you want to have by your side
Ready to ride with you no matter what opposition you collide with
The greatest gift in life is to be able to rise 2 the call
If a friend needs you at all, ask yourself
can they can they count on you
Will you be there through the thick and
thin send word then respond?
Where have you been, some ask they've waited their entire lives
Rise 2 the call with superlativeness no opportunity 2 chance a miss
We must advance, but you don't want to go, no not like this huh!
Well somebody got to go and it might as well be me
Rushing forward, not fully knowing or seeing what the end will be
Continue on, till we're gone guided by our
heart to where we're needed
Twice defeated when man knows his purpose, but afraid 2 go
So much fear, but fear is childish, our destiny is what we're here for
In this war I can't sit back comfortably and let otherz fight
If I believe in freedoms and right I'll rise 2 the call
Somebody got to do it, like I said it might as well be me
Unless somebody else got a better idea!

Seduction

Seduction begin when men enter in
The presence of a woman that has sights on you to befriend
As always unknowingly; you thought your game was to win her
When every time in the end she was the one who forced you to dinner
She made herself available for you to look at
while she pretend not to notice
Then like a fly in a web she would spin captivated all of your focus
You was seduced to ask her, her name and
with a boyish grin came to see
That you might extend a warm welcome,
and in your arms she would be.
But when she spoke of her favorite place to
eat and then drink to her friend
You overheard and ran with what had been a
group of supplanted seductive words send
But you can tell if it was only sport, cause
men are hunted like wild beast
Because of the way she will look at you and
stare or if it's too long then it's a tease
If she looks down then it's one or two things that's in progress
Either she's afraid of finding mutual attraction
or wants to intensify the process
So as she distance herself in connection,
this drives the seduced man wild
And have him thinking it was all his idea, feeling like
the man but really being played like a child
The game is foul in fact; it's not a game she's not playing with you
The mission is pursue, overtake and then destroy your single hood.

Way 2 High

I'm way 2 high, got 2 go, my head is about to blow
I'm down the street from my cousin in the project snow
As I watch them smile sneaky and they beg me to take a pull
I'm way to full off this weed smoke, I choke and drool
I'm told my eyez are super bulged out blood shot red
So I fled running through the projects before I die
I'm way 2 high; I see my life flash by
Heart beating fast as I pass out the front door
Why did I go smoke all that home grown marijuana for?
My man looked like the devil; my thoughts are on a roll
Ohh how he's trying to trick me and capture my soul
All the thoughts running rapid and I can't make them stop
Reality seems in slow motion, I move like a robot
If I can just make it to the bed, lie down and get some sleep
This weird feeling of paranoia death, I'll have it beat
First I need something 2 munch on calm down this weed
Bologna in the fryer pan nope 2 late I got to eat
So it's out the fryers pan and devours the meat raw
Then hurry and lay down just blinking thinking my thoughts
And just like the rush came, next thing you know
It's over and I awake up, that's was a long long time ago
Way 2 high

Dedication 2 Marianne Craig Moore

When the Preacher
buy P@#%y

When the preacher meanders and takes a gander out his peripheral
His Cadillac swings back and forth as a
pendulum, pull up nonchalant
On a pretty prostitute yearning, desires
burning, she needs no seductions
He's so excited as she leans deep inside his
window, asking about money
So the moment is his to relish looking at
round breast, hotel expense at hand
All goes according to plan, since he bought
the condom right after church
Withholding his tithes for the month about
to secretly enter this sacrilege
When he glanced her over yonder his soul relinquished all decency
She slid in the car whispering church boy I'll make you change God's
The solicitor knew she had a victim of flesh succumbed to p@#%y
She was full of atheism, so voluptuous, sex appeal filled the car
It was no more a scrimmage as he indulged in her hellish ways
Paying her meager fee for some scrumptious
p@#%y he's been wanting
Not knowing his spirit would undergo atrophy after this wretched girl
So he entered into her with splendid torrid until they both climaxed
Now it's too late to be cautious talking about please Lord forgive me
Her sweet tender kiss and soft hug was thanks enough for the ride
As she got dropped off back where he seen her slowly walking
It's back to the church to try this religion thing one more again
Ahhhhh hhhaa God is good, he preaches,
but God knows what he did

Wondering will we make it through the bad parts

What we had, and what we have are two different wishes
Paths took in the dark have us guessing and asking questions
So much ambition to get so much more when you're poor
We huddle together, and put our pennies together for a cause
The strange place in life we're trying to go seems brighter than light
Expression of self- preservation and will power is a struggle
I love you and miss you are words we hug to, to carry on
Things went so wrong and not by any fault of our own baby
Committed to share our true destination in life was a must
Trust must come before love, and I trust you with my life
If I become famous then believe me you will be there
Breathing you as air, and my soul is soothed by your presence
It's quiet time and all I can hear is your cute giggles.
I testify to a place we are at now I've never known
Till the end of time, it was shown to me I didn't belong
My place is with love, light and God's grace and goodness
Please forgive me Lord for my sins and my transgressions
The almost truth is we want heaven, but don't want to live right
We don't want to suffer or go through the struggles of life
All we want is pleasure and party time minus God
While drawn to the dark side fighting it tooth and nail
Trying to avoid hell and jail and fall into paradise
The price is the price and it's at times in blood
To get to where we want to go we must go through
something\ how many of us are wondering?

Wretched War

What we go and blame Bush For
We got money for wars, but can't feed the poor
It's us that got to push more
Own our own stores, and keep the pay in doors
Wars never meant us no good
Our cause is understood in our own neighborhood
When I have done all I've could
That's when we should take a hint make a break for the woods
Until then we must fight or die
Not for distant land, but for family close by
Peace got us shell shocked, traumatized, no lie
Why do we just bust out and cry

Youthful Elder

A wrinkly grumpy old man with his pants hanging down
Is about to become confound at the image in the mirror
He looks again, and his dim vision becomes clearer behind shades
As he notice his fade is fading behind his hair line
Thinking his vision was crisp, but almost blind he looks close
Then becomes tickled to death as the jet blackness of his hair has left
And only a bald spot and grey places along with his unfamiliar face
Behind this energetic smile snaggle tooth from old age
The years have left its mark, get sets of tops and bottoms
Replacing choppers, while meat still in between his teeth
Old age over took him in the sprint of his youth
Arthritis and the runs finally caught him in mid-stride
As a cramp from a track star, he hobbles to the side
The race is over as the sun went down on his run on life

Chapter VII

In the depths of my Silence

Jewel: 117: To caution yourself around important people wise, it shows that you are not heedless; To humble yourself in the presence of small people is powerful, it shows that you're not just a common bully.--

Art of Seduction

I have from your seduction a sporadic eruption
Without any touching, mind in a daze body dysfunction
When with you I'll feel my way round, need no instruction.
Without question your presence is a sweet, sweet bliss
Mix emotions comes when you blow me a kiss
I feel this, this, this ohh it's about to come
While elapsed in your tantric embodiment
You make playful gesture while I'm snagged is all I get
Engulfed in your erotic, sirens a passionate lure
My patience has worn thin as a disease your essence is the cure
Will I be able to endure; I'm trying to hold it
Trying to control it, your poise is burning, it's all over with.
It's too late for me; my desire has burst on fire
Your foreplay has touched parts of me, I hope you will admire
I long for my fingers to touch, such and such
I haven't even laid hands on you yet and already miss you so much
I have something very special planned for you
I'm a very eloquent man watch once what I do once I'm through.

Brother's Keeper

Where do two men stand when pride gets in the way?
Looking out the corner of eyes, not finding words 2 say
A display of egotistic character and macho form
Saying stay out my way to keep form causing bro harm
A million dollar born brotherhood in one day reduced to rubble
Screaming at each other in silence, a sign language so subtle
Real dudes do real things but real emotions are in women
Its best friends that start out funny beginnings and tragic endings
But brothers are supposed to get mad then
both have doubts and regrets
Not having poisonous fangs piercing back biting, and vicious threats
With all due respect let me be first to say we all make mistakes
A shaken earthquake rattled within loose feeling mental brakes
As a spring that started as snowflakes, snowballing out control
So is a little chaos that got us at odds with each other soul
Will there be any reconciliation, through words will you forgive
Silence is cruel; we at least say good-by where we live
Like an acorn that becomes mighty as an oak can we grow pass
This small adversity and strengthen a relationship that will last
Different strokes for different folk's obstacles are a mountain climb
After swimming a raging river before
leaving a collapsed bridge behind
I'll always keep you in mind, because I am my brother's keeper
Written 9/29/10 Dedicated to Grayson

Deep within Venus

This holy girl name Aphrodite came unto
the underworld to bring me back
All was black, till she aroused me with an Aphrodisiac
I was a fallen knight, lost at war she said,"
I'll show you the morning star".
But first do you know who you are, 'I said I am Mars
I represent the God of War
While I spoke mighty Thor brought down thunder and lighting
She wasn't frighten, as I stood bold to face beauty in the naked eyes
My earth was deeply drawn where the orbit of Venus liez
This was the rebirth of spring renaissance
happening before the setting of the sun rise
The heat was as ten thousand fires that made me bow down
Between 2 leaning pillars like in Athens
She had the nerve to be tickled, and laughing
as I'm consumed by a burning bush
Now my eyez are wide open like Adam in the
Garden of Eden located in Kush
As sirens of the sea, sing songs that can't be put
into words so is love that imbued the body
I glance up and see two twin round mountains
and question is this where the God's be
In the woman holds the mysteries of the Universe
As mountains of volcanos sporadic eruptions and burst
to the blessed and the cursed for better or worst
It's like showing seasons of fertility in spring daily
So as we met in the underworld me and my girl
Through pleasure and pain to face beautiful
angels and horrendous demons
Carried to the heights of Mount Olympus to Hades deep dreaming
I wake up screaming and smile wondering did anybody notice me

The world receives the reflection off the moon from the sun of Glory
To view directly at the realness of emotions can make you blinded
That in plain sight hidden factors of the
heart can you search and find it
True beauty is more than skin deep, when our eyez miss a whole heap
And truth can cripple us as sometimes it's ugly as Medusa
Acridities showed me what lies beneath hades
and above is paradise of Zeus
From the foam of the sea, which she was
born to stimuli my natural high?
And bring me out of a low state of darkness to a state of bliss,
Atlantis in the sky
When I went deep into Venus

Footprintz

I've walked to the edge of hell with barefoot swelled
On broken glass and hot blistering nails, sublimely in this jail cell
Tell a tell signs show where I've been don't take
my word for it, have a look in my mind
Shush Shush listen closely to all the moans
and endless despair of crying
I've seen the dying eyeing me into my eyes not wanting to let go
He had the nerve not to Believe in God, yet he was
a friend right up to the end of death row
I've become close with the guys that'll never touch the streets again
So they share with me what mental state the time has put them in
Put away the sin, for what, death shall find me
and gobble me up behind these walls
Is what some lifers say, so they look for boys
to break off in bathroom stalls
I've slept in cells the size of beds with toilets by your feet and head
Writings all over the wall, so I add my name
underneath names I've read
I've left tracks on where I've been like footprintz on sandy beaches
Since I'm strolling through this world leave
a mark is what history teaches
Insane brains reign in these cold prison cells, they everywhere
Wait when a female walks by, you can tell by the way they coldly stare
Men gone wild to animal, the saddest thing I've ever seen
Today it's I'm living for the lord, tomorrow
it's getting dollars by any means
So as I travel through and leave a solid print, I hope that last.
I suggest one may follow me, but go further than
me in learning, find out what's on this path

Heartless

When hell got full then the dead started walking the earth
And so at birth a people of night walkers was born here
In the day light, children of the night with no feelings
Please stop with the killings, but we an't feeling no pain
Stains of blood don't phase their kind, they are Zombies staring pass
Corpses laying in the middle of the road we trying 2 pass by
A generation of walking dead spoke of in revelation is now present
You might not notice them, as most are still
locked up in the underworld
Only pop out at night the light is too bright for their bedazzled eyes
Watch them squint with bedroom shoes
on at noon in the corner stores
You can tell how they talk and look; they are not made for-
The day light much, a sense of day time living they've lost touch
Club life, riding at midnight, and watching the sky till dawn
Then dragging on into the dark apartments of where they die
Drunk and high; where they can take their shoes off, sit on the bed
Become bed bound till late in the evening right before dusk
When they hear arguments, squalling tires, and guns that bust
Hood alarm clocks rise up the dead, check miss calls before darkness
Then get dressed up roam in the streets nocturnal living heartless

If I die 2 nite

Entry #3
Wish I could stay longer to enjoy the scenery.
What this means to me, cannot be explained in word.
Dreams deferred, beautiful women, they'll never all let me in them
Send them my greetings, from a placid world beyond
If I'm gone tonight just know I'm alright, I'm ok, I'm ok
My thoughts breath freely, see me now do you believe
Never will I leave, without saying goodbye or fare well
Tell stories of me later if I die 2 nite
We all fight to live longer, but we guaranteed to lose
Allies pick and choose to turn their backs when against the wall
Call me Marvin, if you're really a true friend at all
Don't ever stall to take full advantage of a friend
Then what are we here for, do I snore when I sleep
Pray the Lord my soul to keep if I die 2 nite
I like this world and the pleasures it gives me
Been with many of ladies, ate good as I could
Even gave a helping hand to a few knocked down
Made a mistake or two, now I've found a better way
Hey! Don't cry over nobody if they lived alright
Cry 4 the living in misery, I'm at peace if I die 2 nite

Dedicated to Jesus of Nazareth
The King of the Jews

Judas Blood

See you in hell buddy, you got nailed I got the rope
You bled out I got choked, friends to the end right
Everybody know I'm a fool for money, you're a sucker for souls
Just like the ointment that could've been sold
got rubbed on soles of your feet
Ahhh! Mary Magdalene so sweet using her long precious hair
Filling the air with a delightful odor and the scent of benevolence
Ever since Jesus wept I knew we would always have the poor
My job is to keep cash in store; his was more souls to Jordan River
Since everything cost I'll deliver my pal for 30 pieces of silver
I've watched him get away many times before, the miracle worker
He'll have them running in circles; picture
that Jesus on a cross, Yeah Right!
I must take drastic measures to add to our depleted treasures.
So we at supper, Jesus washing feet then out
the blue he acts like he knows
You told me what I must do go do it quickly, I'm feeling exposed
The whole gang thank I'm going to handle the money business
When he sees me again I greet with a kiss of brother love
Not knowing I just bought myself with silver a field of blood
And it cost my buddy, beatings and piercings at a place of a skull
Both our lives gone, I'm in hell for good,
and you're just passing through
Both of our lives have become null and void, a painful death
You left me just enough rope to hang myself
When you pass through hell please forgive
me, we know not what we do.

Let me be

I see visions of your face start to fade
Taxi!!! Please get me out this escapade
My feelings are hid underneath a shade
Then I get in this car that takes away

We supposed to be friends or so I thought
Us to dispute over petty things brought
Then bring our dream to a steaming halt
I'm not waving no mo, bro let me out

You know I don't believe in people well
He worked his way in and dreams he could sale
His ideas I bought into soon would fail
At least with me, leave me lone, let me be

Lovely Day

It's a tornado watch in my spot 1st came the hard rain
We ducked the severe tropic cyclone called the hurricane
Her name was Katrina, you should have seen her
Down in New Orleans, they brought in FEMMA
It'll take more than FEMMA to rebuild now that's real
Why does it take such tragedy to know what it is to live?
Here comes a Tsunami that flooded up Japan
Close to 10,000 dead or missing as its present stand
The ocean earthquake roared over point 9 on the Richter
Fukushima people fear contaminates in their drinks to make'em sicker
Radioactive elements poured in like shots of liquor
Because of a nuclear complex melt-down, the plot gets thicker
With so much going on in this world of Typhoons
It's been a many moons since I've seen days of doom
No aches and pains, no crisis or catastrophes in my life
No more than this prison for crimes I too must pay the price
God is good and family is O.K what more can I say
Despite what's going on elsewhere 4 me it's a lovely day

My Situation too

Everybody got a situation, but nobody situation is like mine
It's a startling revelation of how few true friends that's hard to find
If it wasn't for my situation you already know I would've been here
It's not fair 2 have out of sight out of mind,
until seen it's no need to care
Shall I bare my situation alone, some stayed for a month now gone on
Some stayed for years and share my tears waiting for me 2 come home
Growing in my situation, and showing dedication on how 2 be a man
Do the best I can and respect the ones who beside me still stand
Some cashed in on my situation the very
moment I lost footing and fell
They rushed in a hurry, gathered all my
belongings and put them up for sale
God has kept me in my situation, because I believe he knows my heart
Some struggle to maintain a consistent relationship,
but you've been from the start
Old friends say they haven't forgot about me,
just got themselves in a situation
I expect then they'll be in and out, but want
extend through the duration
So many have turned their backs on me 2
name them, where would I begin
What a tragic, not so much the situation but
having this situation 2 find out
My real family and true friends

On the Sly

When she gives a certain look in your eye, it's time to reply
Don't deny yourself this curious pleasure its do or die
Hi Lady, Be aggressive but don't come off too strong
Act as if she already belong to you, get fly ask what's going on
It's like she already knows in the first minute
If she's going to give you play, if you're not too timid
Be forthcoming and use unorthodox means if necessary
Ohh she smoke weed, then that's what you need to carry
Share with me, I betcha' she's going to ask you
Become a weed dealer to keeper her happy if you have to
Ohh yeah!! She's party and drinks, bartender keep'em coming
Build her trust, be a perfect gentleman to this woman
Next take her home, and then act like you too drunk to drive
Slur and say can you stay to sober up once inside
When your mischievous self think she's sleep creep into the night
Ease underneath her sheets; be sure to keep it quiet
If she has only panties on this must means she knows
Take off your cloths now whaa-laa you're both easily exposed
Step by step don't rush nothing take your time
Easy- easy now hold it as you work from behind
You're not drunk, matter of fact you in the back grinning
While she lay helpless naked with her head spinning
Even if she tries to throw it back, it's too late good-bye
She took too long you had to go in strong
whether right or wrong on the sly.

Marvin Thomas

Part Time Lover

This scene of rapture, in the wee hours of the night it's eternal bliss
Passionate kisses, deepness and wetness, mixed with hard as rot welder
But when the morning comes this discovery
of unique pleasure is no more seen
They both part ways and it's like this one
night fling has never happened
It's just a weekend thing of joy mingled with tears of having to go
The moment of having enough of one
another is the job of these lovers
To hold each other over through the week
as they go their separate ways
Till the phone call is made on Friday, a trip
over then both are laid in the sheets
Sweet tastes of her enticement, her allurements
only inspire at night time
As moonshine all decency is thrown, and in bed doing whatever
Enslaved in each other's enchanted delusion
sparkled by stars in the dark
Part time lovers don't have the luxury to pillow talk or cuddle
He's softly creeping in so subtle while she lay down getting her rest
Ravished by her breast he slips into the
sheets and tease her secret delights
Both are gratified through the night, pure
satisfaction moments of relaxation
Complete submission and obedience is displayed where they both laid
This love affair is only when they have time to get away and share
Each other remember their part time lovers, consider what's shown
It's best to have someone, some of the time
than being alone all the time.

Quit tearing us apart

Divided we stand, united we fall is all I can recall
From the time before I could crawl very small
They said I'll had to start out playing ball or pump CD's
I find no role model to say the world is mine from my memoriez
Please be pious and devoted to peace can we just get along
Togetherness is the only way to carry on and remain strong
How many of us can imbue our passions to soar from high 2 higher
And not remain at a low estate of degree, the dilemma is pretty dire
Our own rend us, turn us violently against one another with force
With vile affection towards even the purest
of us detesting the very source
Even the most honest and avert, deny unity really ever existed
But It's done out of ignorance and don't know
no better of thought simplistic
If there ever was a time man was all 4 one and one 4 all sorry
We missed it
Stop killing, cause he looked at me, or stepped
on my shoes who you really pissed with
We ripping each other to shreds blowing us to smithereens
From our early teens terror, and madness in families is all we ever seen
Family talk like Willie Lynch had something to do with the divide
The splitting up of nations came from light verses the dark side
The wayz of hell is wide and if it's one for show we all gonna go
I told you so, we need each other, but we
got to stop tearing us up though

School Clothz

First day of school since kids are cruel, I wear my best
Or they'll go poking fun, and I have no gun or Kevlar vest
It's fashion day, everybody that's somebody looks to upstage the other
While another got his 12 gauge in the car, cause he's trouble
He dresses poor, raggedy shoes from last year and toes exposed
Those like him fade into obscurity, because of their school clothz
Who skips the 1st day that's when you appear fresh on the scene
With these new timberlands nobody got and $900 Red Monkey jeans
Have not greatness been recognized in the eyez of my peers
These clothz right here! Yeah I know it! It's tight gear.
Last year clothz gets no rotation till the middle of the summer
And some come in bummy on the 1st day, what rock they live under
They say they'll finish out the old clothz, wear the best last
Too much class I got to fade out, but I got fresh ideas in the stash
My cousin's into fashion too, he's in another town and wear my size
And when they think I'm out of gas, I switch up to unknowing eyez
Now the mean poor kids don't like that, as for me trouble he makes
A sore loser to popularity is he, so he vows my coat he'll take
He pulls out his gun to rob me of my coat outside of school
Now he's kicked out of school for good
because he lacked learning tools
And those are decent school clothz we need for a decent education
Or put us all in uniforms to stop the indigent desperation

Toilet Stool Love

Hey how you ladies doing, as an inmate shouts down the toilet
Through a cesspool of madness his voice echoes to the other end
A new found friend as she listens to him in the toilet on the other side
She brush her hair back before she sticks her head in to speak
What's up fellows as they're held in a female cell down below?
Shouting up the drainage pipe saying erotic things men like to hear
While making wet smacking sounds coming in clear, just imagine
Delivered up also is a name and address to later put with a face
Instead of looks she describes her panties with
lace in this place of confinement
Criminals need love too, for now this will just have to do for foreplay
Till they get carried away and masturbate at the same time
Moaning and making noises till slime runs down both their hands
Now she screams up to her mans, aka her toilet stool friend
Send him messages to send her pictures through her moms
Her voice has charms, so he's up top getting all emotional
Catching feelings causes he hasn't been social with a female for years
Now it appears next step is to tell her he's in cupid's love
He's up above in a b-block cell singing through the toilet
These acts must be pushed out and exploited, toilet stool love

When the Dead meet the Dying

At that deadly moment when the blinding light hit and we meet
It was a sense of overwhelming memories, I'll
never forget, that comes when they greet
I look at cloudy dark gray skies glare from outside my eyes open wide
Peaceful scenery is taken from out a book when one has died
All is in slow motion, golden crisp leaves don't just fall they flutter
And besides the secret winds that rustle and rattle
pine trees, there's a silence like no other
At this rendezvous point is a beautiful smile standing
there with open arms, I mean wide open
A familiar face to usher the way in, uncertainties
vanish when seeing the one I got hope in
I thought when this fairy tale world end, life would
come crashing down to shattered dreams
But now I can't stop smiling by feeling
happier as life flashing every scene
My existence will continue throughout
eternity, she whispered to come
Many think when you're dead you're done, I
can tell you now you're dead wrong
This smell of fresh sweetness and recognizable
odor of a passed loved one
All my nervousness is shoved away and I'm ready to reach beyond
With life harsh realities and its cruel teachings through
experience, first comes the test then the lesson
But I'm not stressing no more, my mind run
wild of anticipation of Allah's blessing
Remember me and if these could be last
words by me you've read and heard

At your side expect me, because I'm coming if you're
going and I'm gone and if you ever truly cared
I'm telling you, I see a family member that's
been gone for a long long time
This is when the dead meet the dying; I'm trying to leave you a sign

Where did I come from?

Baby fresh on the scene from out my wildest dreams
Stuck between two extremes, so I did what might mean
Awake, made noises I learned to call later screams
Frighten by a sudden beam of rainbow spectrum light
Is the nightmare over or did I just arrive on site
As I struggle to open my eyez with all my might
They were closed so tight, now this bright vision of terror
Leaves no question, back again born in this electrified era
Nothing else but prepare the way from cradle to the pallbearer
This nightmare will scare the living day lights out you
It'll make you crawl to a safe space back through
This place you came to before you knew, who was who
What do you do? Close your eyez on this path of true lies
So much disguise to not tell the difference when you analyze
Between the dream world and the real world till we demise
Just like the scent of baby powder rise stink will fall
Think Yall! All of us before we walked had 2 crawl
Jibber Jabber turned to talk, we understood the call
Whether crawling, walking, or running we came from somewhere.
. . . Ask yourself where did I come from

Whispers in the Dark

She massages his broad shoulders gently and caresses him lightly
As her fingers nails crawl down his back as a feather in rhythm
A woman knows timing is everything while
she seduces and butters him up
With her naked warm body leaned against his on the edge of the bed
He sits there relaxed and motionless with
a blank expression on his face
Her nipples brush across his back, and
when he gets chills she whispers
My husband knows about us, or his suspicion will lead to questions
You must do something about him you have to get rid of the problem
She smiles devilishly and whispers, you're not scared are you
She whispers," we have no choice, our hands
are forced, so we can be together
He listen to her describe his abuse and his jealous ways at home
Now her tender voice is in the background
and all he hears is his thoughts
His heartbeat and her whispers if you love me, you'll do it
She whispers," He's crazy and he will kill her if he finds out about us
Her sweet breath blows in his ear and her perfume overwhelms him
Then with a sudden burst of energy, in a rage he grabs cloths
Storms out and kisses her saying baby it must be done
As he pulls off she falls back on the bed and kick her heels up
With her thumb in her mouth and whispers revenge is the sweetest
Joy next to getting . . .

Marvin Thomas

Who got that Crack?

Pull up right there on the block around the back
Where those black guyz are standing at in a pack
Who got that crack is yelled out from the car
Door ajar, here come the full fledge rock star
I know you don't know my face in this place
I'm not trying to get you a case, just give me a taste
I'll suck your . . . come on now don't know what you're missing
Even though I got teeth missing listen, just listen listen
Now you pissing me off, you keep clowning my cloths
Yeah my jeans got holes, and my shoes show my toes
Who do I got to . . . to get a blast of hard
Ok, ok I'll pay you back, I swear to God
Nod off if you want to, you'll get rob around me
While I found your pant pockets to look and see
Where the crack at, get jacked by a stone head
You making idle threats, said give back your bread
Or I'm dead; scare tactics I'm not scared I'll cut ya!
Just get off the bed and leave, live with I stuck ya!
Next day I ask, give me one more blast my last
This time I got the cash, I don't have 2 sell assets
Pass me my steam and put a bolder on the end
Then inhale hard and watch the white smoke rush in.

CPSIA information can be obtained
at www.ICGtesting.com
Printed in the USA
LVHW090512020120
642316LV00001B/61/P